MW01268044

THE POET'S

PERSPECTIVE

The "Poet's" Symbol

The "Pyramid" has always been a symbol of strength, longevity, and wonder in my eyes. In its time, it was before its time.

The 3-dimensions of "The Poet" represent Humbleness, Personality, and Charisma (the working man, the business man, and "The Poet").

PCG Publishing Company
60407 M- Hwy
Bangor, MI 49009
www.pcgpublishing.com

Edited by Kathleen Jackson
Anita Shari Peterson

Cover Design and Text Layout by Tashiki M. Coben

Reviewers:
Please forward one copy of review to publicity@pcgliterary.com

ISBN: 0-9772541-4-3

Library of Congress Control Number: 2005907864

Printed in the United States of America.

PCG Publishing Company books are available in bulk at discount prices. Single copies are available prepaid direct from the publisher.

Contact Mr. Charles Edward Peterson, Sr. at poetryplus4@btc-bci.com

10 9 8 7 6 5 4 3 2 1

PART I

The Mystique of The Poet

The ability to create poetry is a blessing to me
Having the gift to create gives one a great responsibility
Each blessings to create is but a gift to share
Mine focus on a higher power and the cross we bear
You might not possess this same dream or vision
Share the dream with a committed decision
Take your gift as a sword to wheel
I on the other hand use mine as both "sword and shield"
Questioning "society" and "societies role"
Using "acronyms" and "hidden lines" that truth be told
Every "hidden line" accents the "unique" and for "The Poet"

The Spirit

That Dwells

"For God so loved the world, that he gave his only begotten Son, that whosoever believeth in him should not perish but have everlasting life."

John 3:16

I DEDICATE

I humbly dedicate The Poet's Perspective to all **"poets"** who understand that the pen is mightier than the sword. May you use your spiritual gifts and talents to "sear" paths of escape from an unacceptable norm. And to those who partake of this effort and are able to find or redefine their own perspective. I would like to thank, **Anita**, my first born and publicist for all of her help and nudging (pushing). I'd like to thank you for causing me to focus on the book title **"The Poet's Perspective."**

To **Joyce,** my wife, for being there when the rug seemingly was snatched out from under my feet and for encouraging and making me realize I wasn't on it 150 percent. I LOVE YOU!!! *AND MOST OF ALL TO THE* ***"POTTER"*** *FOR BLESSING ME WITH* ...

"THIS WALK OF LIFE"

Where I Am in this walk of life - **You Brought Me**
All That I Know and am blessed to understand - **You Taught Me**
All That I Have be it spiritual, moral, or financial - **You Gave Me**
All That I Am in my worth - **You Made Me**
Yesterday when I was lost in sin - **You Saved Me**
Today as I continue in faith - **You Bless Me**
Tomorrow though not mine to claim - **You've Prepared Me**
And although I could never do enough to be worthy - **You Spared Me**
Forever will I seek your face and I know - **You'll Guide Me**

Acknowledgements

First, giving honor to GOD, who is the head of my life and the true author of all that I am blessed to create and share. I thank GOD for blessing me with the ability to apply spiritual gifts and talents, while working wonders with His Word. And for giving me poetic messages and analogies which relate to, focus on and pinpoint issues that are relative in today's society.

I would like to give a special thanks to my Mother, MRS. ROSIE LEE PETERSON (OLD GIRL), and the memory of my Father, MR. WILLIE EDWARD LEE MOSES MALACHI PETERSON (OLD MAN). Together, they both instilled within me family values, strength of conviction, and that "CAN DO ATTITUDE."

I would like to thank my first born, ANITA SHARI PETERSON (Mother of ALIVIA and ANFERNI). Let's just say she constantly encouraged me to complete this publishing project ahead of my own schedule.

In loving memory to my second born, TANISHA CHARLOTTE PETERSON (Mother of A'MMARY), who gave her life while bringing a life into this world. I know she's in a better place smiling down upon us all.

And to my son, CHARLES EDWARD PETERSON, JR. (Father of ALIAH, KHALIL, TAVON, and SYLVESTER CHARLES), my namesake and academically gifted young man — THE BEST IS YET TO COME.

In my efforts to raise three children as a single parent, I honed my character and cleared my focus so they could learn by example, which helped to steer me BACK IN GOD'S HANDS.

To my brothers, Willie (Rasmiah), Oscar (Rosella), Clarence (Rosa) and Ulysses (Linda); to the late Benjamin Peterson, whose artistic genius and painting have yet to be recognized; and to my only sister, May Frances

(Dwayne), I love all of you unconditionally and you all have helped to fulfill this dream spiritually, mentally and physically.

I would like to thank my wife, Joyce L. Peterson, for understanding that I need five more minutes to write and for loving me unconditionally. Let's just say that we will be on a honeymoon every weekend during my book tour.

A special thanks to Mrs. Mae Lucas, Mrs. Doreen Archibald Smith, Mrs. Renee Jones and Cheryl Swanigan-Sisson, your dedication and commitment to Poetry Plus Incorporated is very much appreciated. I'd like to thank my niece, Tashiki Meawona Coben for the superb layout and design of The Poet's Perspective.

And thank God for my church family at Gospel Tabernacle Baptist Church. My unwavering faith has given me a solid foundation and a new beginning for the hard times, lonely times and moments of doubt.

I'd like to give special thanks to two young poets, Joylynn M. Jossel and Marc Lacy, for supporting my first endeavor The Poet's Perspective. Your constant encouragement and enthusiasm has made me smile on more than one occasion. Thank you from the bottom of my heart.

Lord I thank you for the strong, yet humbling ART that strengthens me, and for the FRIENDS at the end of the tunnel, who enlighten and allow me to bring forth the spiritual gifts that have been buried for FORTY YEARS.
Charles Edward Peterson, Sr.
"The Poet"

3:16

First, giving honor to God who is the head of my life, I am The Poet, Creator of Rhythm and Rhyme through fantasy and reality from past, modern day and future times.

I am Executive Director of Poetry Plus Incorporated, an organization dedicated to the dream, the cause and a vision of a better day. I speak in schools, colleges, churches, open mikes and correctional facilities. I recite to a myriad of listeners about faith, hope, peer pressure, drugs, guns and alcohol, as well as having dreams, visions and goals.

The Poet's Perspective is doctrine laded, opinionated and a highly rated, respected effort. For I come as one "Crying In The Wilderness" *"Trying To Open The Eyes Of The Children Of Man Before They Are Harvested By Minds Of Destruction."*

GOD CALLED PREACHERS

GOD SENT TEACHERS

GOD SENT PROPHETS

&

GOD SENT POETS

BEHOLD THE BLESSINGS OF

"THE POET"

EXCUSE ME, MY BROTHER, IT IS NOT ENOUGH to just read **THE BIBLE. THE ISSUE** is about **FAITH and WORKS.** In order to gain eternal salvation, **YOU MUST BE BORN AGAIN.** It is good that you study to show yourself improved, but know that what you read convicts you, so **WEIGH THE COST.** Yet, I encourage you to **FEAR NO EVIL,** such as **THE STAIN OF DEATH,** as you endeavor to understand **THE A B C'S OF CHRISTIANITY.** You might want to do as I in asking the Lord to **ORDER MY STEPS.** I don't know what you say **WHEN YOU PRAY,** and maybe, **YOU DON'T KNOW LIKE I KNOW** because, unlike me, you may not yet realize what God has done in your life; but it's easy for me to say, **LORD, I THANK YOU. IN THE BEGINNING,** God planted a seed, which is clearly explained in John **3:16;** that encourage men and women to **HOLD ON.** For this time, **TWILL SOON BE PAST,** as did the time when intercession was made for us and it came to a point when He said, "Father, forgive them **FOR THEY KNOW NOT** what they do."

And, as we endure now under the blood, I see us as **THE 99 & THE PREACHER,** enduring the loss of the Shepard, yet striving to do HIS will. We know that **WHEN HE COMES CALLING, (THE DEATH ANGEL),** we are all under the blessed watch of **THE WATCHER.**

PRAISE GOD

THE
POET'S
PERSPECTIVE

"THE…"

IS USED TO INDICATE

UNIQUENESS

"A POET..."

A Poet is one who is especially gifted in the perception and

expression of the beautiful or lyrical

"PERSPECTIVE..."

A perspective is a mental view or outlook:

As to look at the past to gain a better perspective on the

present

The Poet: A Biography

Charles Edward Peterson, Sr., was born on May 9, 1950 to Rosie Lee and Willie Edward Lee Moses Malachi Peterson in Benton Harbor, Michigan. Being the fourth child of seven children, he vividly recalls using his writing as a vehicle to escape into his own world. He wrote poems and short stories in his younger years to express his thoughts, goals and dreams. And his Blue Trunk he made in his wood shop class, as a freshman in 1964, was the holding place for his creative work.

After high school, he married his sweetheart, and as a result of this union, fathered three children. After seven years of marriage, Charles was left with three children to raise as a single parent. Anita Shari, Tanisha Charlotte and Charles Edward, Jr., were his responsibility, but with the help of family, friends and the community (**THE VILLAGE**), he raised three healthy children.

During the early morning hours, The Poet wrote extensively and placed his creative work in his Blue Trunk. Over the years, his Blue Trunk became filled with over one hundred poems and it was at this time he decided to publish his first book in 1993, "The Poet Speaks—Chasing After A Dream." His first work was dedicated in memory of his beloved daughter, Tanisha Charlotte Peterson, who died minutes after smiling and holding her newborn son, A'mmary, in 1991.

The Poet is a civil rights activist, community leader and humanitarian. His community service includes reciting poetry at correctional facilities, Christian youth camps, and participation in marches for unity awareness and atonement. He is very active in his church as a deacon, Sunday school teacher, and male chorus member.

He proudly holds the rank of black belt in the martial arts and has many trophies displayed on his shelf from tournaments. Charles enjoys playing chess, Bid Whist and serving God. And you may find him on the golf course in a city near you, because he is an avid golfer.

The Poet's love of creative writing through his poetry is a reflection of his passion for the written word. Authors he admires the most are James Baldwin, Langston Hughes, Nikki Giovanni, and all unknown poets with a message.

Forty years later, The Poet and his Blue Trunk have survived many disappointments, heartaches and pains, but the poetry written during this forty-year span is a testament of faith, humbleness and spiritual guidance. And The Poet has just begun to speak!!!

The Poet is but a voice crying in the wilderness trying to "*Open The Eyes Of The Children Of Man Before They Are Harvested By Minds of Destruction.*"

"I'VE BEEN LIKE AGING COAL, BUT SOON I'M GOING TO SHINE"

Seeds Of Wisdom (An Ode to The Poet)

When The Poet speaks....
Seeds of wisdom become planted...
Dormant freedom forests become enchanted...
...enchanted with the bliss that blew in through
the hiss of the wind...as The Poet utters words
of uplift, mediocre thinking gets set adrift...

For spiritual elevation is the destination The Poet
endeavors for all to achieve...
When your heart's door is open, look in, now believe...

Amazing is the taste of grace as it flanks "Wretched" Sound,
Sweet is the feat of release as eternal freedom will never cease...or keep
one bound....
As The Poet speaks peace...
Fields of communion are irrigated, nurtured and leased...
Leased out to those who want to protract with the angle of
interaction...which is a distraction to fallen angels as they aspire to
disguise what is righteous....

Finally...

The Poet is a virtuoso of taking colloquialisms and transforming them into
rejoicing rhythms...
Rhythms that the rhythm less can dance to
as they romance their way through this thing called life...
He influences everyone to have the divine behavior...just like The Blessed
Savior, as we were developed in His likeness, God is so good that your chest
should have a tightness, a tightness indicating that your spirit is lighting
this candle called agape...and if you don't have The Bible...get a copy...

Poet, you have spirit stronger than nuclear fission, as your heavy influence is
cast...you are handling your mission...

From A Poet to The Poet...Much Love....
Marc Lacy - 05

THE
POET'S
PERSPECTIVE

The Spirit that Dwells

IT IS NOT ENOUGH

IN THE BEGINNING

HE

3:16

THE 99 & THE PREACHER

FOR THEY KNOW NOT

THE A-B-C'S OF CHRISTIANITY

THE BIBLE

THE ISSUE

THE WATCHER

EXCUSE ME MY BROTHER

ORDER MY STEPS

YOU DON'T KNOW LIKE I KNOW

SEED

FAITH

WORKS

WHEN YOU PRAY

WEIGH THE COST

HOLD ON

LORD I THANK YOU

FEAR NO EVIL

YOU MUST BE BORN AGAIN

THE STAIN OF DEATH

TWILL SOON BE PAST

WHEN HE COMES CALLING (THE DEATH ANGEL)

Sometimes, there is no reason to add to or take away from a creation or work. Just like it makes no difference, at times, how much you have or how much time you've invested. That which you face is often awe-inspiring and you come to realize, even with your very best:

"IT IS NOT ENOUGH"

Though I give to the poor, and have joined the followers of The Word
Though I lift His name up before the masses, telling what I've lived, not just heard
Though I give my tithes and offerings, and avail myself to do good deeds
Though I pray with fervor, or sing until the angels take heed
It is not enough
Though high men might know my name, and give me great acclaim
Though my bank accounts may have measure and my barns the same
Though I study to show myself approved, that I can rightly divide The Word of Truth
Though I've been on the battlefield for ages, having joined in my youth
It is not enough
Though I'm baptized by water, and partake of the blood and bread
Though I hold an office in the church, and have a title found in "The Word"
Though I visit the sick and shut in, and aide the widows and orphans as well
Though I boldly proclaim to be a Christian, and profess Heaven over Hell
It is not enough
Though I attend service (most) regularly, and try to convince others to do the same
Though I fellowship with the brethren, and lift my hands to praise His name
Though I ask The Lord for guidance and to daily walk with me
Though I try to be obedient to the word living, accordingly for other men to see
It is not enough
For, if I look back from whence I came, adding all the things I do, try, or have done
Then think of how much The Lord gave in giving His only Son
Then I think of my salvation and how much it truly cost
Thinking how my Jesus gave up The Ghost nailed upon the cross
Then I know, although we believe our efforts worthy,
Often finding the going rough, I need but to think of Jesus to know
It Is Not Enough

Excuse your toes, but as it's said, "If the shoe fits, wear it." Sometimes, it takes adding it all up to subtract self from the equation. For it's not about how much you gave, endured, or how long you've been doing it.

"THOUGH I'M BAPTISTED BY WATER AND PARTAKE IN THE BLOOD AND THE BREAD"

Way back, beyond the phantoms of the mind, was created "The Beginning." And man has questioned and scrutinized it with his vast, limited wisdom from generation to generation. And Man has pitted scientific evolution against spiritual creation. All scientific explanations are found to be inconclusive, conjecture, presumption and theory. All based on man's evaluations and deductions.

The written word is a living document that starts off with, "in the beginning" (hint). It speaks of a creator who created "The Heavens and The Earth" and divided the waters from the waters, created all the animals, birds, fish and creepy crawly things of the earth. And formed from the dust of the ground "Man" and blew into him the breathe of life.

"IN THE BEGINNING"

In this world of what came first the chicken or the egg
The big bang theory or the primate evolution misconception
Beginning has been questioned and opinionated off the gauge
Was there a cosmic explosion in the cosmos back beyond the eons?
The thing that created order and started the eventual cycle of time and life
Word to the alleged wise who believe this theory and offer explanation
And spout scientific rationalization supporting their theories of relativity
The explanation and rationalizations are all somewhat unique
Word of "God" though, supports awe, purpose, harmony, balance and creativity
Was there by chance a big bang, and if so, who supplied the power?
With these explanations, doesn't something have to power nothing?
God has set "His Word" among us and, how over man's interpretation it tower
And who among us can deny that all things that originate have to have an origin
The complex configurations of universes, galaxies, worlds, and man "happenstance"
Word of "God" documents the events of creation as "in the beginning," for men
Was there any other need for documentation other then, for questions there are answers?
God is the answer for in the beginning was The Word and The Word was with God.

Take a look around you and behold what man has done to and what is with his limited wisdom. Everything that was created by man had a beginning; an origin from something. Then look no farther than your own solar system and see constant balance in distance, revolving planets with revolving suns and moons, and know that in each there is purpose. Can this kind of order come from such a destructive force (which had to get its power from nothing)?

"I CHOOSE GOD'S WORD!"
"THE COMPLEX CONFIGURATIONS OF UNIVERSES, GALAXIES, WORLDS AND MAN HAPPENSTANCE"

Often times, I've gotten caught up in my meager successes, and in times gone by found myself taking credit for the accomplishments that I was blessed to achieve. I know I'm not the only one who has come to realize at a crossroad in life that it was not me but:

"HE"

He lifted me
He prodded me on
He hued my will out of stone
Then He took my strength
After making me strong
And He brought me through
That I would know it was He alone.
He taught me that pride goes before the fall
It's not the swift, nor the strong
But He who endures through it all
And He humbled me, to hear His call
I've been up the rough side of the mountain
Lord knows it was a long haul
He guided, enlightened and protected
I slipped but He wouldn't let me fall
He opened my eyes so that I could see
That it was HIM, HE
Instead of me

When you come to that fork in the road, and your limited ability and knowledge leaves you incapable and void of understanding; remember HE is The Author of new beginnings.

"HE TAUGHT ME THAT PRIDE GOES BEFORE THE FALL

IT'S NOT THE SWIFT, NOR THE STRONG

BUT HE WHO ENDURES THROUGH IT ALL"

When the last accepted sacrifice was offered up, and the stench of sin yet lingered before "The Almighty God" the existence of all mankind was held in the balance. Purity was what it would take for the salvation of mankind. Through all the sacrificial offerings, wonders, and miracles mankind did not truly know how much "GOD" loved man. Until "HE" made the "Supreme Sacrifice."

"3:16" (The Sacrifice)

For whatever the reason he paid a great debt
God yet looks over us and hasn't given up yet
So it's up to us, for eternity is ours to share, for we're
Loved far beyond anything man could compare
The reason "He" was willing to die for men, a
World of trouble a world of sin
That "agape love" "He" has within, and
He knew, we'd no longer be able to save our own souls
Gave us an avenue from which "He" yet controls
His son was willing to pay the cost, for
Only "He" could save our souls, which were lost
Begotten of the "Father" with all power in hand, yet willing to become
Son of Man

Well that's an answer to a "S.O.S.," a beacon in the night, and a light at the end of the tunnel. For mankind had become as salt that had lost its savor. But down through the generations "a Star" did shine. For Purity was what it would take to save mankind. The "Only Begotten Son of God" rose to pay the cost and was allowed to give up His Life upon the Cross.

"For God So Loved The World That He Gave His Only Begotten Son."

"He knew we'd no longer be able to save our own souls"

In my walk of life, I have lived and experienced many blessings which I have been able to document. And the role I played in this real life episode of tragedy, faith, and a parallel fulfillment surely strengthened my faith. After the passing of our shepherd (Pastor), the search was on to find another shepherd. And after doing so, I was challenged in a way by the new first lady of the church to write a poem for the new pastor's birthday. And in doing so, I documented the events that had unfolded, but all things may not be, as they appear to be. As I am honored to be able to share with you:

"THE 99 AND THE PREACHER"

Caught up in the darkness - yet not giving up the fight
Following a vision of hope and spiritual might
Brought out of the darkness, back into the marvelous light
    For GOD sent a preacher
There was a flock without a Shepard, a people in need
99, without that 1, (which was lost) to lead
The 99 stood together, believing God would intercede
    And GOD sent a preacher
Fear and confusion caused others to doubt
But they were on the outside not knowing what it was all about
The 99 stayed their course, believing GOD would work it out
    And GOD sent a preacher
The word itself is a teacher
To help create in us a new creature
Although there's many things "The Word" feature
How can you hear without a Preacher
The devil lingered folly his pleasure
Uncertainty was applied, time to measure
But they held on "Faith" their treasure
    And GOD sent a preacher
For those in the Faith, I'm sure you know it
You must be bold, yet humble, and unashamed to show it
To aide you, GOD sent teachers, prophets and poets
    And GOD sent a preacher
The fulfillment of GOD'S Word was "HIS" major intent
Yet, the preaching of the gospel caused others to resent
But the bringing of salvation to those who'd repent
Were the main reasons The Preacher was sent

Few are called, but many come
But to no other sacrifice would GOD respond
For none was found worthy, but His Son
So, GOD sent a PREACHER

All things aren't as they may appear to be in life, we must sometimes hang in there to see what the end's going to be.

"FOR NONE WAS FOUND WORTHY BUT HIS SON. SO, GOD SENT A PREACHER"

In His Word, He said, "His ways are as far from ours as the East is from the West, and as surely as it's questioned, who is Man that he should be mindful of." We, as Man, questioned His first coming and what he would do when He arrived. We did the "unbelievable" but in His forgiving way He pleaded to "HIS FATHER" saying, "Father, forgive them":

"FOR THEY KNOW NOT"

Father, I come in this darkened hour, asking you to
Forgive this deed of "mortal men," yet look on
Them with thy (merciful) forgiving power
For I come into the world to die for their sin
They do not understand, neither do they
Know that I've lived to die, that they may live again
Not to fulfill this (world's) interpretation of
What they thought would come to be for
They know not what is the Father's will, nor
Do they realize they are fulfilling my "destiny"

The Word says when He comes again, even "the dead shall rise." And it won't be any mistaking who He is the next time because the trumpets will sound and at the mention of His name every knee shall bow. And we now know why He came; for it's said in "His Word" that I've lived to die so that they may live again. But He actually went beyond His effort on the Cross because He petitioned His Father, saying:

"FATHER FORGIVE THEM FOR THEY KNOW NOT WHAT THEY DO"

Sometimes we have to go back to our ABC's to understand the true jest of the matter. And to first visualize it in such a simple format as the ABC's was interesting, but to have it come to life one letter at a time in tandem is more than meets the eye.

"THE A B C's OF CHRISTIANITY"

Almighty/Alpha
Bread/Blood
Christ
Doctrine
Edify
Faith
Grace
Hallelujah
Intercession
Jesus
Kingdom
Lord
Martyr
Noel
Omnipotence (unlimited or infinite power or influence) Omega
Prayer/Peace
Quintessence - (Perfect example- Purest form of....)
Repentance
Savior/Salvation
Trinity
Utmost
Visions
Wisdom
Xmas
Yoke
Zion

To recite the ABC's of Christianity touches one to have a personal revival. So, if you're one of those, kick off your shoes, "Holy Ghost" filled, run down the middle of the isle Brothas or Sistahs, I recommend that you don't recite this while driving (or in some cases riding), in heavy traffic, operating heavy equipment, or during inclement weather.

"CHRIST

JESUS"

If you want to take a trip and need to find the best route, use a road map, atlas, or nowadays, you can plot your course from your vehicle or computer.

If you need a plumber, an electrician, a carpenter, or the name of that restaurant with those smoking barbecue ribs, use the yellow pages or call 411.

If you want to find out about the country, how it began, and who's who, locate a history book and search for United States. But, if you want to know about GOD, and how He made something out of nothing, and separated the waters from the waters, about the creation of all life including man, or how God came down in the flesh as Christ Jesus and walked among men, read:

"THE BIBLE"

The beginning of time is recorded there within
History of the universe, the world, and the conception of men
Established is the dominion of man over the waters, the sea and the land
Blessed to be created in the image of "God" he stands
Instructed not to eat from this tree, for they'd surely die one day
Beguiled by Satan, they were tempted and did disobey
Life after Eden is then recorded, (in the Chronicles), of The Word
Each generation with worthy input is then heard
The record shows how God gave instruction to man
Greatest came when Christ brought salvation in hand
Recording of the generations were then B.C. and A.D.
Of all the efforts of life, Christ becomes the key
History in The Word is unique, giving instruction then and now
Known by the Commandments that we yet endow
To the children of man it describes "Judgment" in a future time
Man yet has a choice as with the tree that will determine a life sublime

This, by chance, is your ticket to those pearly gates, for which we should study to show ourselves approved. Now, in doing so, you will be doing a good work, but work needs to parallel faith. And by studying The Word, we increase in faith.

So, if it's in you to seek beyond who you are, (or who you think you are), and what you have. To find or even question, where it all began, how we got here from there, how there's life after death, and why there was a ransom paid, and even get a glimpse of "Heaven" then read THE BIBLE.

"THE GREATEST RECORDING OF HISTORY KNOWN TO MAN"

Yeah, I know some of you have issues, but if you'd study just a little bit more, you'd know that it rains on the just as well as the unjust. But, it just doesn't seem right sometimes to see someone you know that isn't even trying to do God's will be, or appear to be, so successful. But don't you know that everyday is another test of time, and it's really not about what others have, but about where your values are and where your treasures are stored up. Now, that more so is:

"THE ISSUE"

Why the turmoil, why the test
Do we need to suffer to find success
God need not justify by no means
Let us seek out our visions and our dreams
Bad vibrations, misinterpretations questioning why
Things go awry no matter how hard we try
Happen without warning, with no reason or rhyme
To the just, to the righteous, to the saints who are trying
Good and evil shall suffer righteously
People have always questioned the issue of the odyssey

Being one to question the issue of the odyssey signifies that you are a believer. And it would be nice, if that by being a believer, everything would be like the fulfillment of The American Dream. But you know HE doesn't work like that, in every life a little rain must fall...

"WHY DO GOD LET BAD THINGS HAPPEN TO GOOD PEOPLE?"

Have you ever thought you saw something amid the stars or had the feeling you were being watched? Thought you saw someone, but no one was there in the shadows, in the glare of the sun, or just beyond your focus. Well, the book I read tells me that someone is watching and we will be held accountable for the deeds done in this body.

There are many ways to sin: greed, lust, idolatry, hatred, and a host of others we've invented and re-invented. Here is an opportunity to step outside of the circle and look within yourself so you may judge and not be judged by the report of:

"THE WATCHER"

How often have I traveled to this far and distant land
To behold the progress, advancement, and the degradation of man
I see his efforts all throughout known histories span
And I wonder how he made it so far
With total destruction long being so near at hand
I stand within the shadows naught but to observe
Measuring the blessings of life, mankind did nothing to deserve
I evaluate potential, understanding and growth

Compare the present unto the past, documenting them both
I am cloaked within their midst and often applaud
By their many, many sacrifices, I'm left awed
But in a twinkle of an eye, I'm bewildered and don't understand
As I witness another act of man's inhumanity to man
I watch and I behold, as the desires of the flesh takes control
As the demonic one (without a battle) possesses another soul
I watch in astonishment as pearls are cast among swine
As the wisdom of the word is ignored by most of mankind
I watch as they turn on each other over the mere color of skin
Not rationalizing that all flesh is sin
I wonder if each of you, as representatives of many generations
Could plant the seeds to change the cultures of many nations
For I stand at the pivot point, marking time as it passes by
Wondering how many more blessings will come from on high
Wondering if mankind will ever realize, and if so, in what generation
It's only that which is done for "Christ" that will bring salvation

Can you see it? Do you realize that our children are absorbing it, testing it, and often before many of us are even aware, living it? The information, the standard, the moral character, the examples you set, the attitude, and the things you allow to be considered acceptable are passed on to the leaders (the children and their children) of tomorrow.

There is a verse which somewhat holds us accountable for future events; "we should train up a child in the way they should go." How else can we, who can see the need for change, play a part in an effective change, except through the culturing of the seeds of tomorrow?

"I WONDER IF EACH OF YOU, AS REPRESENTATIVES OF MANY GENERATIONS, COULD PLANT THE SEEDS TO CHANGE THE CULTURES OF MANY NATIONS"

To all who have been blessed by the spirit, you must stand boldly before family and friends, or you will never be able to reach out to the stranger along the way. We are truly blessed to be children of the King, but know also that we are soldiers of the King.

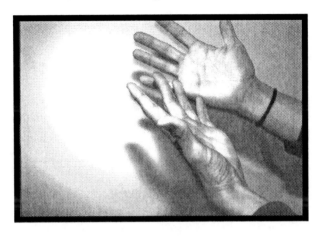

"EXCUSE ME MY BROTHER"

Excuse me my brother, for you might not like
What I'm about to say.
But it is in my heart that I should say it anyway
For the Lord may ask me come "Judgment Day"
Did you go among the lost, or speak righteously
To those you called Friend, or did you just
Stand by and watch
As old Satan did them in?

Did you try to bring any lost sheep to the fold
Or just claim to be a Christian,
And play a saintly role?

My Brother, I love you, can't you tell
And I hate the thought of you burning in Hell.
Take heed while there is time
For the "gateway" is yet open,
But the day of the Lord is near at hand,

For he shall come as a thief in the night
Bringing with him everlasting life.

The Fire shall precede him though,
And only the righteous will ever know.
Take heed, my brother, change your worldly ways
The world is in trouble
We're in the "Last Days"

For those who know, it's not always about the child of the King, but while there is time, it's about the soldier of the King. For it's not just your responsibility, it's your duty, to go among the lost and encourage them to the narrow path of salvation. For it's written, "it is His will that all men be saved."

"DID YOU GO AMONG THE LOST OR SPEAK RIGHTEOUSLY TO THOSE YOU CALLED FRIEND"

Belief, purpose and direction are all wrapped up within your faith. And once you have faith, it will, let's just say, adjust your level of belief, enlighten your purpose (in time), and give (or with some, stir us in) a better direction. For when one has faith they pray to the spirit to:

"ORDER MY STEPS"

The light that shines and lights the way
Steps ordained from the miry clay
Of saints and sinners we behold
A transformation more precious than gold
Good is the desire this quest to fulfill
Man is created to do "His" will
Are you blessed with a purpose to achieve
Ordered by a higher power in which you believe
By "The Spirit" that blesses and judges men
The one who guides your steps, and on whom you depend
Lord of Lords who keeps us on one accord

To find that gut wrenching, know it in your heart and mind and have that can't anyone tell me any different faith. My, my, my that's seeking to be steadfast in the faith. And that's more than just talking; it's yielding that the spirit can align your walk. For:

"THE STEPS OF A GOOD MAN ARE ORDERED BY THE LORD"

Everyone has a story to tell. And it's within the bounds of your life's experience and the avenue or avenues of choices made that define you in part and what you choose to believe. Those life experiences surely have brought you, at one time or another, to a point of need (spiritual, physical or financial).

If that is so, maybe you are one to boldly testify that:

"YOU DON'T KNOW LIKE I KNOW"

You might see me praying in the house of prayer
Don't understand the reason why I seem to always be there
Know that everyday is a blessing and that we should ever praise His name
Like or not our circumstance, we should praise "Him" just the same
I have my reasons why I praise Him, many you wouldn't understand
Know there are ways "He's" blessed me that makes me His greatest fan
What must I do to get you to lean and depend on Him like me
The "Savior" has blessed many for many blinded eyes now see
Lord of all creation far beyond what we think we may control
Has he not looked beyond your faults and made a way for your soul
Done many miracles, worked wonders of which I can attest
For you don't know like I know the reasons I profess
Me, a lowly sinner, has truly been blessed

To marvel at life is to question its beginning, to experience death and wonder why, to stand helplessly by and watch a friend or loved one suffer, or have compassion on the less fortunate or pray for a lost child. To desire to see the world become more of what you believe, The Lord would have it to be. And in the midst of the hoopla of everyday living, a prayer is answered or may be unbeknown to others, a small miracle is made just for you. (Ask, Seek, andKnock in prayer).

"YOU DON'T KNOW LIKE I KNOW WHAT THE LORD HAS DONE FOR ME"

    We are entrusted with the task of rearing, or as our forefathers would say, of raising our children. And not just raising them, but training them up in the way that they should go and as we lead and teach, putting in our own perspective, we're often blessed. Blessed to reap what we sow, so water and cherish the:

"SEED"

He gives us seed to scatter around
But it's up to us to work the ground
Through "His" grace we are profound
And from our efforts we shall abound
As we manage each fertile row
When we water it shall grow
And come harvest we do know
We shall reap that which we sow
With each waking hour we are blessed
To improve on that which we profess
For each day is but another test
We must take before we take our rest
Striving in this world to succeed
Often deprived of want and need
There are many things we see and heed
As an enslaved mind is rarely freed
So each life is as seed and field
We cultivate, we sow, we reap, we till

From but a seed are our lives fulfilled
We live to die to live our fates are sealed
So soil and seed intertwine
Bound by a cycle of marriage and time
Cycle ending always beginning anew
All from a seed that took root and grew
So from death we shall live again
Sown with yet reaped pure of sin

Of course, you know the best way to train a child up in the way they should go is to lead by example. That "do as I say and not as I do" thang has played out. Because our children and our children's children are a whole lot more educated to life then we were at their age. With the influx of computers, the internet, x-rated T.V., the "big screen," CD's, DVD's, and near to life video games; you practically no longer need to have that Father to Son or Mother to Daughter "coming of age" chat anymore because, in some cases, they can tell you a "thang or two." That being said, if you don't teach them and try to instill decent values and moral character; then they will be forced to face society alone and make grown folks decisions at an early age. Rear the seed.

"BUT IT'S UP TO US TO WORK THE GROUND"

"SO SOIL AND SEED INTERTWINE"

There will come a time in your life where you'll have to believe. Believe beyond your own capabilities; believe beyond your education, your strength and your wealth. Believe in that which is unseen, believe for a family member, a friend, or because your fate hangs in the balance. When things are out of control or out of our control is when we realize who is in control. In believing we learn to have:

"FAITH"

For whatever the struggle
We must learn to endure
Walk the walk of faith
By the way of the light that shines pure
Faith in the unseen, guided by love
And hope and trust in that which is
Not of this world, but from the heavens above
By blessings of which we bare witness of
Sight unseen through faith and love

Come in from the dark do not be deceived. Know that we are children of faith and not products of fear. It's been said, "as a man believes so he is." And that "fear defeats more men then any other obstacle known to man." Faith is the antidote for a sick soul as is one who's caught up in society's role. Trusting only in self and that which they can see.

"FOR WE WALK BY FAITH AND NOT BY SIGHT"

To make that walk up front and confess your faith, and then to be submerged in baptism is truly commendable. But it's only the beginning. For we must put on the whole armor, study to show ourselves approved, and let our light shine so that others may see. "Whew," that's a lot of work right there, but He said, "my yoke is easy and my burden is light." And, He also said, "I'll put no more on you then you can bear." And by knowing that there is a "weight restriction" on all that comes your way, (even though you often feel just "a tad bit" overloaded), you now know that you can handle it. So, have "faith" it:

"WORKS"

Works of the heart
Without the acknowledgment of the spirit
Faith only in your ability to achieve,
Is shallow to say the least
Dead to the spiritual world of which many believe
Faith yet in that realm
Without action on one's behalf
Works only for a season unattended
Is barren as the tree that gives no yield
Dead to it's purpose dead to "He" who ascended

To have faith is to believe. See how short and sweet that is. To have faith is to believe, and to believe in Him, is to also have faith in His Word. Surely, there is work to be done, for He said in His Word that He desired all men be saved. And although you are a child of God, you are also a soldier of the King and are duty bound by the works of The Word. For:

"WORKS WITHOUT FAITH IS DEAD...FAITH WITHOUT WORKS IS DEAD"

I am one of those who believe that everything isn't written in stone and that the die is cast and fate is already foretold. Because, in the first place, we were blessed with the right of choice by "The Almighty." And secondly, we are blessed that prayer changes things. So BELIEVE:

"WHEN YOU PRAY"

IF you worry after putting it in "The Masters" *hand*
YOU'RE smothering your blessings with doubt
GOING through life's trials without a clear plan
TO put it plainly, you don't understand what prayer's all about
WORRY after prayer shows the lack of faith of man
DON'T give prayer that through faith fulfilling route
PRAY without doubt or you may be casting your blessings out
IF you believe in the power of prayer
YOU'RE covered by blessings in times of despair
GOING down on your knees to pray
TO humble yourself and ask the spirit to guide your way
PRAY in season and out, when you fill worthy, when you doubt
DON'T let the power of darkness have its say
WORRY not for "God" will make a way

Ask, seek and knock are truly good directions. But if you don't first believe, then the spirit of doubt will plague you. And that will trigger the fear of being unworthy to petition unto The Most High. And where there is doubt and concern without belief there is worry.

"IF YOU'RE GOING TO WORRY DON'T PRAY"
***
IF YOU'RE GOING TO PRAY DON'T WORRY"

Oh, no one said it would be easy. And the greatest temptation known to man is woman (and vise versa). And you know you are in warfare against the power of the air. And the stronger you become in the Spirit, the more you will be tempted in the flesh.

So, before you give in to temptation, consider the strides you've made. Secure your armor, keep the faith, and by all means:

"WEIGH THE COST"

Moving to the tempo of a rhythm unheard
Body language gyrating to each unspoken word
A familiar tune being played in the corner of the mind
Summoning you back to a life you've now left behind
Back to a time where you knew not the way

But you've come a long way from back in the day
Yet temptation is ever present to the children of men
Trying to deny them the victory they must win
Yet it's packaged and presented so well
You're lured by its features and tempted by its smell
And slowly but surely you remember a line or two
That would possibly pull this vision closer to you
But as surely as you remember the walk
And how to suavely talk the talk
A voice causes you to hesitate
A voice you've learned to appreciate
Asking you to stop to weigh the cost
Of what would be gained and what would be lost
But you can read the signs and tally the score
But you're not the man you once were
So you summon up a needed and worthy prayer
To lead and guide you beyond the tempting glare
And as you deny yourself and give praise
He blesses and promise eternal days

But maybe you're more tempted by that "mean green" so that you can get that, (as this generation would say), "Bling-Bling." Or maybe your weakness, (because temptation once honored becomes that weak link in the chain), is what used to be your drug or drink of choice.
But whatever is (or was) your weakness, remember you're not the person you once were, you're a new creature and the "GOD" that you serve is a momentary GOD.

"SO YOU SUMMON UP A NEEDED AND WORTHY PRAYER"

If you've come to that point in life where you realize we are in the midst of Spiritual Warfare, if you've studied, or have truly begun to study to show your self improved, and if you believe in Angels, demons and Heaven and hell, then:

"HOLD ON"

This old world is filled with sin
The devil and his demons are deceiving men
They're in a battle that they can't win
Don't let them steal your soul, before "He" comes again
We are Soldiers, on a "great" battlefield.
You are in a "war," pick up your sword and shield.
You're fighting an enemy that you can't kill
He'll destroy your Faith and "corrode" your will.
You'd think by now we would have learned
"He" promised us, "He" would return.
"He" came before, was treated like a stranger
Lowly born in a manger.
"He" lived. "He" died.
"He" met the price we had to pay
Then "He" went away to prepare a place for us.
And Vowed "He" would return one day.
Hold on my brothers and sisters. Hold on.

And the war wages on. Just as another effort is made to open the eyes of the children of Man before they are harvested by minds of destruction. For some are blind and cannot see, some are proud and will not see, and some are beguiled and shall not see.

"DON'T LET THEM STEAL YOUR SOUL BEFORE HE COMES AGAIN"

Have you been through something? Have you attempted and failed? Have you come to the point where your best was far from good enough? Where there was no one left to turn too, and you find yourself unexpectedly, fervidly, deep in prayer? Maybe you're too strong, to proud, or maybe you're just not "down" with prayer. Been there, done that, so keep living. When those situations arise where strength of character or strength of conviction does not heal, cannot cure, or right a wrong. When the light at the end of the tunnel is always around the next turn. And if you can look back and realize you have been blessed than you might want to say (as I):

"LORD I THANK YOU"

For all the wonders you allowed me to see
All the miracles you made for me
For all the faith you instilled
The confidence and the will
For the courage to be strong
Through the many things that go wrong
For the Darkness in my life
And the "Beacon" that shines so bright
For the fellowships that I've known
And those who've prodded me on
For the family I was "Blessed" to share
All the love and the care
For the many times I have failed
In my effort to prevail
For the times I've been misunderstood
When my intentions were good
For filling the emptiness I've felt inside
After loved ones have died...I THANK YOU!
For if my life had not been so diverse
I'd probably have faired worse
And would never have known
All the "Blessings" you've shown
LORD I THANK YOU! ! ! !

To get to where you're going shall be a test of time. For the best laid plans of mice and men, shall always be subject to snares along the way. To come to know how and why you were able to make it through the pitfalls in your life is to give thanks and praise.

"FOR ALL THE MIRACLES YOU MADE FOR ME"

"Fear defeats more men than any other foe known to man." I wish I could take credit for that statement, but it was one of those pearls I picked up on this walk of life, from the teachings of "the elders" or from "the school of hard knocks." When one professes his faith, sheds the old man to become a new creature in "the spirit" then the spirit of darkness threatens, often by temptation, lust of the past and doubt. But hold fast to the faith and know that "God did not give us the spirit of fear" and:

"FEAR NO EVIL"

I know the power of darkness will cast a shadow over my life
Will try to cover my sunshine with clouds of strife
Fear is his biggest weapon against the children of faith
No, I will not give up because he makes my walk unsafe
Evil is always present with those who dare to believe
For its purpose in life is to damn and deceive
Thou are a safe haven, a guiding beacon of light
Art Thy Word as but a shield against fear and strife
With the power of faith I know that I shall succeed,
Me and all those who follow your lead

Becoming a "New Creature" in the Spirit isn't like having a total makeover. Because a makeover may call for a clip and cut, nip and tuck, or maybe a polish and file. But becoming a new creature in the spirit is a total makeover of the heart, mind and the body from the inside out. And fear is superseded by faith.

"I WILL FEAR NO EVIL FOR THOU ART WITH ME"

With each day, the word comes closer to fulfillment. Each of us are in a position to be held accountable for our deeds and actions on Earth. Our mortal being is constantly being challenged by the ways of the world and if you want to earn salvation:

"YOU MUST BE BORN AGAIN"

You'd think that we could reason
Our knowledge being so keen.
Understanding at a level the world has never seen
Maybe we are reasoning that our moral character's fine, but
Unless you truly believe
Soon you'll be left behind
Time is surely passing, it's time we changed our ways
Believe in the scripture, know we're in the last days
Each of us must answer for our earthly deeds
Before the "judgment" seat of God
Our hope is Christ will intercede
Realize that only through master
Not through worldly deeds
All our souls are saved from sin
Given eternal life and supplied all our needs
Again I must reiterate
It's time for a change
Now is the acceptable time if salvation you hope to gain.

Surely the last days are upon us and it's time we put our houses in order. For judgment waits in the wings of time, and if your main goal in life is to gain salvation, you must survive the test of time. And You Must Be Born Again, it's so written.

"YOU THINK THAT WE COULD REASON OUR KNOWLEDGE, BEING SO KEEN"
"UNDERSTANDING AT A LEVEL THE WORLD HAS RARELY SEEN"

I look at society and often wonder how we got so far off track. How did we ever get to the point where there was something worth more or was more precious than life. And now we publicize death as a lure for the games our children play. We dramatize it on the big screen, T.V., radio, books, and every other avenue of our so-called entertainment. Then we wonder why there are those among us who don't seem to know reality from fiction. And to think it all started because of God's approval and disapproval (and a brother's jealousy). Behold,

"THE STAIN OF DEATH"

Once upon a time
Beyond the canyons of my mind
Was created a man - He was "Pure"
But once introduced to sin
He was tested again and again
To see how much he could endure
He spread his worth all over the land
Having dominion from span to span
Except in "Eden," where he began
For he was cast out - never to come again
For his sin nature, it grew and grew
Him daring to cast off - it daring to pursue
Til, atlas innocence cried out - from beneath the soil
For jealousy had caused a brother's blood to boil
And with his hand, his brother he slew
And the stain of death, the earth first knew
The "stain of death," from a brother's hand
Is twice "the curse" from where I stand
There's no better reason - in "His" plan
To truly "Love" your fellow man
Other than "Thou Shall Not Kill"
For it is The Father's Will
Then to look back on when innocent blood did flow
An cleanse this "stain" from long ago

Our children see it everyday; it's factored into the games they play. It's often played up to be macho, glorified, and in some places, the acceptable norm. But "God" forbid. And if your willingness to play the devil's games causes you to fall prey to self-destruction, know now that you are blessed with choice. And you're held accountable for your actions. You must protect your future, protect your freedom and protect your dreams and goals from being caught up in "society's role." And by all means, "know" there is so much value to what may appear too many to be, at the time, a worthless or non fruit baring life. Because with each tomorrow, there's hope and God often puts us through something that we'll be able to testify to by going through the trial of fire.

No matter what your situation or circumstance it's written, "Thou Shall Not Kill." And it's going to all come back to God's approval or disapproval. And:

"THE STAIN OF DEATH, FROM A BROTHER'S HAND, IS TWICE THE CURSE FROM WHERE I STAND"

Wow, if we'd but take the time to step out of the circle just every now and then, we'd probably stop taking so many things for granted. Like life for instance, we see it consumed on a daily basis in so many numerous ways. It shocks and horrifies us momentarily but nowadays if it doesn't touch home or real, real close to home; it's usually only a "shake of the head" and a "mumbled exclamation." But, if we'd just look back on the time lost or spent, maybe we'd grasp a better hold onto the allure of a day, an hour, or the moment, for it:

"TWILL SOON BE PAST"

Only time will complete the test
One day alive, next day at rest
Life is such a fleeting thing
Twill end often before you achieve your dream
Soon, and very soon, judgment shall come
Be "ye wise, be ye ignorant, or be ye undecided," as some
Past can reveal what you have achieved
Only "His" mercy thou can save by confessing that you believe
What's important now is that you're now aware
Done is the time when you were ignorant and didn't care
For now you've found the key to salvation
Christ is that key, without "Him" comes damnation
Will you now chose wisdom and travel the road less trod
Last, as in live, your life, for the "glory of God"

Sometimes life escapes us even while we are yet among the living. You know, like when we get caught up in that day to day grind. And your whole life is filtered through that 9 to 5 whichever numbers that you must answer to weekly. Don't get me wrong, let's have a moment of clarity, because having a job or a career is most commendable. What I'm talking about is when that job or career, the seeking of that degree, or striving for that rank, or even being a parent, etc., has got you. Or the not having a job or career, or not being in school or service, or not being a parent, etc. has got you. When you are so caught up that you bypass this event, miss the game, the play, or the program. You forget birthdays, anniversaries, give up on family, friends, your original dreams and goals, and even on God. Working to enjoy a future reward and not enjoying today's presence.

"ONLY ONE LIFE TWILL SOON BE PAST ONLY WHAT'S DONE FOR CHRIST WILL LAST"

Surely, as each day is a new beginning, as the winds of time seems to carry blessings and curses. The Death Angel rides on the power of the air. Bringing with him a roster dated from near the beginning of time. If the grim reaper were to dock at your door today, would you be able to say, let the work I've done speak for me. For we all must stand accountable.

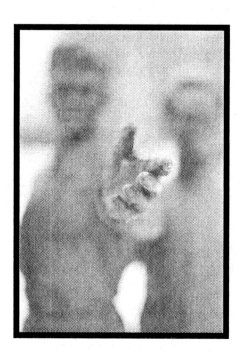

"WHEN HE COMES CALLING"

When the Death Angel comes
Your time is not negotiable
His Mission and purpose
Is the collection of Souls
For the mystery of life isn't death
But the usual untimely arrival
Of the administer for whom the Bell Tolls
Have he no ears to hear you complain
No compassion for your pain
No sympathy for those you're leaving behind

Lo his is but a "unimpeachable" task
Fulfilling the "Fate" of all mankind.
We've watched him pluck up family, friends and strangers
As one would flowers from a field
It matters not your age, color, status or gender
For in his book, your "Fate" is already sealed.
There is no negotiating the "Final Curtain Call"
For he comes in all seasons with a "Quota" to fill,
concerning us all
Prepare for him by the work that you do
For, as sure as he has come for (your loved one or friend)
He has an appointed time for you.

Well, there's the blunt reality of another area of life (death), where man has no control over the inevitable. It can seemingly be slowed down, but it yet is fate. For it's written as sure as you were born, you shall die. Or to put it in the words of a friend, "none of us shall get out of this world alive." But there are those among us who believe there is life after death. For surely as there are believers, there are those who do not believe, those who are undecided, and those who are halted between the two opinions. Oh, but surely as the Death A ngel shall come, so (it's written), shall come Judgment, for the deeds done in this body. Undecided or misled, evaluate, re-evaluate, choose, believe, for:

"THERE IS NO NEGOTIATING THE FINAL CURTAIN CALL"

PART II

The Reality

Of The Day

"Children have never been very good at listening to their elders, but they have never failed to imitate them."

James Baldwin

SOCIETY'S ROLE is not meant to be negative; it is not intended to, or is it, pointing fingers or calling names. It is addressing situations, circumstances, and causes which affect the harmony of today and the built-in factors that carry over into tomorrow. Society's Role relates to, in part, the negative influences and causes that emulate and eradicate the strides made by generations gone by of a people and a nation.

SOCIETY'S ROLE is a combination of time spans, events, and in many ways, the expected reaction of a given situation, social structure or percentage there of. It takes us by another's will, against our will and into free will.

There have been many unknown soldiers (and known soldiers, some who've marched to the beat of a different drummer), who have won many battles against corruption in our society, yet have fallen prey to the inter-struggle and entangling of society's role. We have allowed ourselves to become a nation who'd rather incarcerate then educate, who would elevate the right of free speech over prayer, and on more that one occasion, allow the will of a few to outweigh the votes of the majority. Surely, we stand, as a nation of intellect, power and influence undeniably equal to any threat of war that may come upon us. But it has been said, "that if we were to defend our nation the way we fight the war on drugs, we'd soon be speaking a foreign language."

Lastly, a principle worthy of uniting or that boast equality for all, is managed or maintained only by adhering to a sound foundation; this one being of the people, for the people and by the people.

SOCIETIES ROLE

BUT WE GO ON
BUT WE GO ON (Translated)
THE A-B-C'S OF SLAVERY
THE DRUMS
THE RHYTHM OF THE OARS
FAR BEYOND THE DISTANT SHORES
RACIST
PREJUDICE
THE PLAN
I AM THAT I AM
KING
W .W. D. K
DRY, DRY, TEARS
NO JUSTICE NO PEACE
HOPELESS
WHEN I WAS A CHILD
BACK IN THE DAYS
THE OLD SCHOOL
THE WAY IT USE TO BE
ITS COME TO THIS
SOMETHING WITHIN
IT TAKES COURAGE
YOU'RE OUT ON YOUR OWN
ABSTAIN
FATHER
REALITY
MORE THAN MEETS THE EYE
SEE AND HEED
SO MANY TEARS
CORNERED
HARD TIMES
LITTLE BROTHER
IS THAT MY CHILD
LITTLE JOE COOL
STATS
DRUGS GUNS AND ALCOHOL
THERE ARE NO CHILDREN HERE
CRACK COCAINE
LOOKING BACK
CIRCLES
CHILDREN OF THE PAST

THE SEEDS OF MAN (A HERITAGE TO RECLAIM
THE GENERATION OF CHANGE
IF NOT US WHO, (IF NOT NOW WHEN)
WHAT WILL IT TAKE
I WONDER....911
ASK NOT
ALI
I WISH YOU WELL

If by chance I happen to miss stepping on your feet, I'm truly sorry. Let your mirror be a witness against you. For, "But We Go On" is a reality check, and since none but ONE was perfect, we all fall short:

"BUT WE GO ON"

We've begun to look like, act like
And even think like, "clones"
Sad empty faces with no minds of our own
Caught up in Society's role, selling our bodies
Our children, our minds, our "souls"
(BUT WE GO ON)
People rely on capital gain
All caught up in a social strain
Reaping unnecessary pain and going down the political drain
(BUT WE GO ON)
Because progress is the way
It makes no difference if we've forgotten how to pray
Making plans for tomorrow that we may never see
Putting stock in a future that may never be

(BUT WE GO ON)
Dreaming and scheming, trying to get ahead
Forgetting to be thankful for our daily bread
Getting so "big headed" forgetting who we are
Where we came from and from how far
(BUT WE GO ON)
Playing the daily lottery, the horses, rolling the dice
And stacking the cards, trying to beat the impossible odds
So what my neighbors starving, I'm not my "brothers keeper"
Not even aware of the "Grim Reaper"
(BUT WE GO ON)
Some of us think we've got it made
Others crying the blues because someone rained on their parade
You might wonder where all of our wisdom has gone
Try your neighborhood "rest home"
(BUT WE GO ON)
We've become creatures of habit, "easy prey"
You can set your clock by another's routine each day
But alas, someone else sets theirs by yours and so on and so on
(BUT WE GO ON)
Meeting each sunrise as though it was ours from the start
With malice, misunderstanding and deception in our hearts
Just a repetitious organ that merely complains
A systematic phenomenon of the Capitalistic strain
(BUT WE GO ON)
Existing in life as though we are figments of
Someone else's imagination, dancing to the music that moves
Our bodies, encloses our minds and shatters our goals
Make nightmares of our dreams and destroy our "souls"
"How long - like this - can we go on?"

If I happened to step on someone's feet whom couldn't quite stand the pain, please attribute it to my sense of responsibility and obedience, and try to find it in your heart to forgive me. For I believe, "if each one teach one, each one reach one" then maybe we can stop

"Existing in life as though we're *figmentations* of someone else's imagination"

If by chance I happen to miss stepping on your feet, I'm truly sorry. Let your mirror be a "witness" against you. "BUT WE GO ON," IS A REALITY CHECK. And since none but one was perfect, we all fall short:

"But We GO ON"
(Translated)

(We've begin to look like, act like and even think like clones)

The reasons we're beginning to resemble something manmade, seemingly unable to make our own choices, is because the expected is often our avenue of choice. We prostitute our bodies, exploit our children, corrupt our minds, and sacrifice our souls.

We tend to rely on financial gain, which allows us the stress and strain, to try to fit into a higher social order. No matter how much pain we seem to endure, while others play politics with our every effort.

But because we've bought into the capitalistic desire of progress, many other things are seemingly unnecessary; it doesn't even seem to matter that we no longer pray.

And we so often invest into a tomorrow of which we hold no guarantee, plotting and planning how to supersede "the norm." Not even showing thanks for the many blessings set before us. Making a few strides in life, disassociating ourselves from our roots, and burning down the bridges that brought us this far.

We now openly invest in games of chance, the daily lottery, the horses, the dice and the cards. Fulfilling the prophecy that "a fool and his money shall soon depart." It doesn't matter that as we cast our pearls to swine, that there are those who are truly in need all around us. Nor do we rationalize that we are doing the work of a corrupt will.

Sleeping a sleepless sleep from which one rarely ever awakens. Living an empty life except for material sakes. Out of site out of mind, a good man is hard to find, only a few really trying.

Many of us, having found a measure of success, think that we are ahead of the game. While others swear that this big dark, parade drenching, cloud shadows them. It kind of makes you wonder if there are those among us are "stuck on stupid." And how much un-harvested wisdom is there in the senior citizen homes. We've become predictable "victims." We very often run parallel to another's unconscious norm, but are actually only reflections to the "encroaching monitors of time." And, so it is for the "watched and the watchers."

We greet each day seemingly unaware that someone paid a ransom for our being. Approach it with our hearts filled with selfish, misaligned, and often, corrupt intents. We consistently mouth-off, mumbling and grumbling, amidst the humdrum of society. Notably, we are the most powerful and unique creature God created on this earth. And we've been reduced to a "mere statistic." Fulfilling our state of being as though conjured up in the subconscious of another. Gyrating to a rhythm that activates our bodies, condemn our minds, and refutes our reasons for existing. Allowing the powers of darkness to shadow our hope and capture the essence of our spiritual being. (But we go on).

If I happened to step on someone's feet that couldn't quite stand the pain, please attribute it to my sense of responsibility and obedience. And try to find it in your heart to forgive me. For I believe "if each one teach one and each one reach one," then maybe we can stop.

"Existing in life as though we're figmentations of someone else's imagination"

Surely, the events of this era in American history has had a drastic effect on the social, economic, political and educational imbalance of society, as we know it today. And although history outlines and details that which once was lawful and acceptable, it is yet the catalyst that often fuels the fire of racism. In the eyes of some, it has become, "I wasn't there" and "that was then, this is now."

To others, it is that which burns in the pit of their being. And although, try as they may, they often, intentionally or unintentionally, draw from this well. It's not all because many gained prominence because of this era, but because every now and then, you run into someone with that same ineffable demeanor.

"THE ABC's OF SLAVERY"

Abductions/Abolitionist
Burnings

Castrations-Cotton
Death
Evil/Equality
Freedom/Fear
Graves/Gall
Hatred
Illiteracy
Jungles/Just Because
Killings
Lynching
Murders
Nigger
Ostracized
Property (human)
Quota
Racism/Rape
Slavery/Shackles
Three-Fifths Human
US/USA
Victims
Whippings
Xenophobia
Yearn
Zero

Lest we forget, "that was then and this is now." Lest we forget, truly, the events of our past have played a part in the relevance of today. Surely, there were good people on both sides of the matter; abolitionist, the "American Civil War" and many average every day citizens (Black & White) who fought and gave their lives for what they believed in and duty.

And we should teach our children from where we came, knowing there was good and bad in the midst of calamity. Lest we forget.

"SLAVERY"

I can often hear their faint echoing. I can almost feel the sensation and the trembling of those bound by the beat, an unmistakable rhythm, that's loud, alarming and warns of sails in the distance, on the horizon, or in the bay. Slaver ships, tall ships with big sails, coming to pick up an ebony cargo. Ushered into shore by the constant cadence {Boom, bubaboom, bubaboom, bubaboom, ba} of the:

"THE DRUMS"

Boom, bubaboom, bubaboom, bubaboom ba
Boom, bubaboom, bubaboom, bubaboom
Boom, bubaboom, bubaboom, bubaboom, ba
Boom, bubaboom, bubaboom, bubaboom
The Drums - beating out the rhythm
Of the return of the slave ships
The chained ones are whipped, beaten, drug
And hurried to the sandy shores - herded like stock
Blacks - from many different tribes, stuffed and crowded
Onto the ships into the belly of the huge vessels

Unto at last they were filled, overfilled
And the "ineffable," had once again been recorded
For after all the blacks, were loaded on the ships
The remaining "Blacks" were paid for their "Ebony cargo"
And one of the greatest "Black on Black" crimes
Once again occurred - for many captured
Enemy tribesmen were sold into slavery
By their own kind
Boom, bubaboom, bubaboom, bubaboom, ba
Boom, bubaboom, bubaboom, bubaboom,
Boom, bubaboom, bubaboom, bubaboom, ba
Boom, bubaboom, bubaboom, bubaboom,

My mind reveals this hidden rhythm, riding and lingering, unwilling to fade through the ages of time. It surges through my veins, and hindsight finds my forefathers moving to this rhythm, unaware that it's paralleling their everyday every move. Today, its rhythm may have changed somewhat, but it can clearly be seen in many of those caught up in society's role. They exhibit the slave mentality, and openly destroy one another. "Once a man twice a child, what goes a round comes a round and history repeats itself."

"For many enemy tribes men were sold into slavery by their own kind"

Some minds can't stand to go back beyond yesterday, let alone reflect back on how many of us got here from there. But take a moment and come with me (not to fuel the fire of angry, but to realize a strength within), on a journey from the Motherland to the Land of Milk and Honey, and listen to the

"RHYTHM OF THE OARS"

**They came,
They followed by the scores
As though summoned,
By the "rhythm of the oars."
"Sharks"
Filtering through the waters,
Waiting for the "inevitable" the "ineffable."
Then it happens one oar stop
The "rhythm" is broken
For whatever the reason,
Lack of stamina, rebellion, sickness
"Splash"
The waters churn with the "frenzy " of "Sharks."
Momentarily the vessel leaves the throng behind
The ritual, the inevitable, that which was "ineffable"
Was factored in above the "quota."
Stroke, Stroke, Stroke, can't you "hear"
The rhythm of the "Oars"**

Way back on the dawn and sunset of another day, the great tree grew another branch. For its seed drifted from shore to shore. Rooted, budded, blossomed and bared a fruit worthy of the ground it purged. Revealing strength, character, endurance and the ability to adapt, even after much seed sifted to the depths of the open sea.

"The ritual the inevitable, that which was ineffable"

Many vessels crossed and crisscrossed the waterways of the open seas. Many docked on the shores of the Motherland, returning to their homeports with new seed, fabric, commodities, and her most precious non-commodity, her precious Black Souls. But, as sure as many, many, many Black Souls were lost in route, in an effort to be free; every now and then freedom was won on the open sea. But, alas, all things aren't as they may appear to be. Come and let's take a look back:

"FAR BEYOND THE DISTANT SHORES"

Far beyond the distant shores there sails a ship
Which has once again harvested the Motherland
Its cargo is not her diamonds, rubies, or gold
But her most precious non-commodity
Her children, her seed, her precious black souls
Somewhere there floats a ship off course and adrift
Its captain, its original captain and the majority of his crew
Losing the battle for freedom on the high seas
Alas have been sown asunder
By the unbelievable desire of its former cargo to be free
Its new captain and crew, ignorant
Of charting the stars, reading the wind,
Manning the sails and battling the waves
Can all but stay afloat in the vastness of the open sea
And the frail boundaries of a new found freedom
Somewhere far beyond the distant shores
The battle for freedom was once again won
But alas it was but a momentary victory
Because lack of knowledge subdued the victors
For now they are slaves to the will of the open sea

And another battle is won in the ongoing struggle of freedom, but the war wages on. "Yet," let the lessons learned in the past cultivate a better understanding of the present and the future. For it is written, "For my people perish for lack of knowledge." For many times, we gain the victory, but can't operate the vessel of success.

"Because lack of knowledge subdued the victors"

RACIST

Ignorance and fear, more often than not, the majority is judged by the deeds of a few. Unfortunately, it's common in all races and you can't always tell who's a:

"RACIST"

Radical	Extremist
Anti-social	Harmful to Public Welfare
Color stricken	Prejudice
Inept	Foolish
Stereotypical	Unimaginative or Over-simplified Conceptionist
Thin Skin	Easily Offended

Beware of this person's (his or her) philosophy and forceful will. Relate your point of view to your children, other members of your family and friends, just as you would or should about drugs, guns or alcohol. Hopefully, you'll tell them as I; surely each man should be held accountable for "his own actions" but one's whole race shouldn't be held accountable for the deeds of one or a few.

"Extremist"

"Harmful to Public Welfare"

PREJUDICE

Have you ever been accused of being prejudice? Or know anyone stricken with that horrible disease of the heart and mind? Prejudice has no color, no foundation on which to stand, it can only be pasted on by loose lips, lying tongues, weak minds and fear.

Here's how The Poet broke it down with Webster's blessings.

"PREJUDICE"

P - Phobia - **A persistent and irrational morbid fear**
R - Regarding - **Relating to**
E - Equal - **Competent, adequate**
J - Judgment - **Evaluation**
U - Unilateral - **All one-sided**
D - Devotion - **Dedication**
I   - Interracial - **Among races**
C - Communicated - **Made understood by others**
E   - Epidemic - **Effecting many, contagious**

Being prejudiced is to be subjected to a persistent and morbid fear; relating to competent evaluation; an all one-sided dedication among races; made understood by others; effecting many; contagious. Fear and hate are the most powerful demons in satan's army. But we don't walk by the spirits of fear and hate, but by Faith and Love.

"A persistent and irrational morbid fear"

Doubt, disrespect (for self and others), jealousy, insecurity, rebellion against acquiring knowledge, physical and mental abuse one to another, "15 minutes" of fame, and a high rate of "black on black crime." There are those among us engrossed in an ongoing pattern of living that borders on a slave mentality and "genocides." WHY?

"THE PLAN"

Way back on this walk of life when bound and not free
The world began to get smaller that all eyes could see
Not wanting to be forever connected with slavery
And having failed in preventing blinded eyes the victory
A plan was concocted to keep those who were not free
Bound in a mock web of alleged freedom for an eternity
Congregating together to discuss this simple, but dastardly plan
How to format it, institute it and maybe always keep the upper hand
The plan was instituted to help keep a lower working class
And to keep those who were no longer ignorant from moving up too fast
To keep unrest in their spirits, and every day walk of life
To turn the bitterness back on themselves increasing in their strife

By eroding the family structure, removing the head of the household
Giving women full charge of the children and taking on the man's role
Dividing by religion, social standards, politics, and even color
The plan once initiated would simply turn the subjects upon one another
A plan, a plot, a scheme, a conspiracy against their hopes, goals and dreams
An effective plan that would have lasting effects as so it seems
So when you approach your brothers, tell them of "the plan"
That we may start a backfire to replace hate with love throughout the land
For surely the way we live "the plan" is "yet" suspect
Gamely exterminating nationally our culture in deliberate effect

Did Malcolm X hit the bull's eye when he said, "you've been hoodwinked and bamboozled?" Have we been purposely channeled into a sub-standard existence? Questionable. Probable. Imaginable. And, that if believed, is truly ineffable. Where to from here? Can we change to the degree of facing the image in the mirror and turning to a higher power (surely we can't right this wrong alone)? What is needed?

Humility, forgiveness, self-confidence, vision, the courage to once again dream dreams of fulfillment, to live for a cause, stand for that cause, and strive to train up the next generation and set standards of morality, inspiration and focus, for a better future for all men. To strive within the boundaries of the system to make the legal system more of a justice system.

These are but a few of the stepping-stones needed to rebuild, not only a royal linage, but also the kind of character needed to lead a nation.

**"A plan was concocted to keep those who were not free
Bound in a mock web of alleged freedom for and eternity"**

THE
POET'S

PERSPECTIVE

Have you ever wondered why the Creator of life created Man, and for what purpose was life created? If so, in questioning, have you questioned and tried to figure out your relevance. Questioning, "who am I?" Searching through your values, principles and heritage, to summarize just for self, or to someday stand on your soapbox and proclaim....

"I AM THAT I AM"

Who am I
I'm the Spirit of reality and truth
Love and compassion
I'm the hope of yesterday past
Of sacrifice and blood
I'm that flower in the midst of a great debris
Who the old ones knew, once watered would bud
I'm that desire to be free, in the cotton fields of old
The quivering from the lashes that anguish
That knowledge that something is missing
Deep down in your Soul

I'm that surge, in life that made you shout out loud
That through it all and come what may
I'm black and I'm proud
I'm every Father's Desire, and I counter every Mother's sorrow
I'm the reason you should train up a child in the way he should go
The reason you should vote
The reason you should help those who can't help themselves
I'm the reason why you should reason
That except by the Grace of God, there stands I
I am that I am
I am the hope for tomorrow

In the world's population, the history of each individual is surely diverse, with each race having traveled different paths to get here from there. There linger many reasons why (at times) we should expound on who we are as individuals, and to the best of our ability, what we have contributed so those who've not walked a mile in your shoes will know you (and yours) better. And then, maybe even you shall learn to appreciate your people and yourself better. And after reflecting on how you got here from there, learn to proudly state, I am that I am.

"I'm the hope of yesterdays past of sacrifice and blood"

Some men live life from day-to-day, accepting each day with any and all of its challenges that pushes and channels the majority along. But every now and then come some who have visions and dreams. Those who do not go with "the flow" but themselves create channels through the established norm. Among those came, one marched to the beat of a different drummer, a visionary, a dreamer, a drum major for justice.

"KING"

He was assassinated in his prime
It seems he died before his time
But he lives on in my mind -- KING
He lived for peace so it was for Peace he DIED
But he had climbed the MOUNTAIN
And viewed the other side
And in so doing he had seen the fulfillment of His Dream -- KING
Things aren't as good as they ought to be
But thank "GOD ALMIGHTY"
They aren't as bad as they used to be
Thanks largely to the efforts of Men
Like the late great "Dr. Martin Luther King Jr." -- KING
The KING, is dead, long live the KING
Let's scale the MOUNTAIN and view his DREAM
In memory of him, let Freedom Ring -- KING
His life was an example that others could see
A Crusader for Peace that All Men Should Be Free
He Marched. He Spoke. He sat in. He was Arrested and Abused
Some Men say he was Belittled and Misused
But no Man is YET to fill the SHOES of -- KING
He's more than but a MEMORY
He's a MARKER in My past
And thank "GOD ALMIGHTY" He's "FREE AT LAST"
"FREE AT LAST", "FREE AT LAST"
I thank "GOD ALMIGHTY" at least He's "FREE AT LAST" -- KING

Well, there it is, the way it came to me (how I remember it, not how it was told to me). To leave a legacy of such stature is to set a standard that is to live for, to the degree that to live by that standard he believed it to be one worthy to die for.

"A crusader for peace that all men should be free"
Surely, he marched to the beat of a different drummer, and through his efforts and many others of his time, change and changes were brought into being. Basic changes that enhance the quality of life, but when a new standard is somewhat forced on the majority by an oppressed minority, then it is usually that which is accomplished by great sacrifice. And surely should be safeguarded and strengthened by those who are the main benefactors of such change.

Great were the changes, great were the sacrifices, and great were the anticipation and expectation for future generations.

Having been raised on the cusp of change and seeing great leaders address the need in different ways with different intensities, and having witnessed the living tragedy of man's inhumanity to man, I look upon the quality of life today and often wonder:

"W.W.D.K. SAY"

What would Dr. King say:
If he could see us today
If he could see how far we've come
If he could see how little we've done
About the plight of the world today
About the segregated war on crime
All the minorities doing time
W.W.D.K. say:
About the politics of the day
About the circles that intertwine
About the "Dream" he left behind
About the racism that still exist
About the legal slavery in our mist
About the lack of respect we have for self
About a "cause" set aside on the top shelve
W.W.D.K. say:
About many of the youth of today

About all the ground they've lost
By following visions that's false
About the respect they've lost over the years
About the morals that's disappeared
About the many reasons why
Our young people die
About the role models they choose
All the blessings they lose
About a misguided generation
About the future leaders of our nation
W.W.D.K. say:
About the family of today
About single parent homes
Where all the fathers have gone
About how we're caught up in society's role
Submitting willfully or un-willfully to its will
Forsaking our "dreams and goals"
About the leaders of today
About the efforts they've made
And the roles they've played
The slight of hands political charade
What Would Dr. King say:
About what we need to do today
To help change a slave mentality
Planted before we found our own reality
To help bring us back in line to be our brother's keeper
That we may rise to the mountain
And not in the valley sink deeper
To help us to stop accusing everyone else
To help save us from ourselves.

The cause nowadays, at times, seems to be more so about the "bling-bling" than bringing together the many facets of an ever-diversifying world community. And it seems the efforts and sacrifices of our fathers, forefathers and the many leaders (and unknown leaders), have brought us to a point in life where our fathers were. But we must look within ourselves and know there can be no progress without change.

"To help us to stop accusing everyone else to help save us from ourselves"

What triggers an inhumane event? Is there a pattern? Are we learning in any way how to combat these horrible acts of man's inhumanity to man. What will it take to heal the racism, bigotry, and eradicate prejudice from our land? How long will there be reasons for:

"DRY, DRY, TEARS"

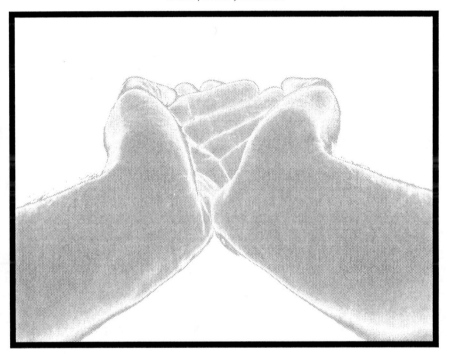

Silent figures swaying gentle among the leaves
Hanging at ropes end solemnly in the trees
Lonely watchers sobbing, crying dry, dry tears
Eyes no longer able to secrete water
Lord, we've been crying four hundred years
Earlier there was a gathering lashes were dealt out
It was meant to be a lesson the superior ones taught
You'd say a slave owner could rightly rebuke his own
But the time is the "nineteenth century" slavery has
long been gone

Lonely figures sobbing, crying dry, dry tears
Ravished and raped, lusted and feared
To weak to stand, don't have the strength in their knees
Their loved ones swinging harmoniously in the breeze
Because others feared their color like a disease
They hung them high in the trees
They took their life because of their fears
Fears they've had near four hundred years
Fear of their own extinction, their own demise
By a process that they begun but didn't realize
A process that begun through slavery and hate
Disobedience to God and Gods will and rape
Lonely figures sobbing, crying dry, dry, dry tears
Justice closed an eye and no longer hears
Lord, we've been crying four hundred years
How do we convince them to get over their fears?

In an age and time when to turn on the six o'clock news is to wind up plummeting head first in the midst of a kidnapping, drug or gang related slaying(s), a horrid hate crime, or a terrorist bombing or execution. It's no longer unusual to see those dry, dry tears for those victimized or closely related to today's headlines. There are many, many reasons to cry dry, dry tears. One is that the unfortunate day-to-day inhumane incidents that others suffer are viewed and tolerated to some degree because we are not affected. And it's not our concern until they do.

"BECAUSE OTHERS FEARED THEIR COLOR LIKE A DISEASE"

As sure as the struggle goes on between good and evil, also goes the struggle between justice and injustice. How often has justice fallen through a loophole? Or been determined by the amount of monies, prestige or social status one party had or didn't have? We are in a generation where many of those empowered to make the laws, break the laws. And those empowered to protect the laws, themselves, disrespect the laws. We must make provisions in the law, that the weight of the law then falls heavier upon them. But as sure as two wrongs don't make a right, we must learn to work within the law to change the law, and make the system more of a justice system than a legal system. We will not go quietly into the night. For we hold these truths to be self-evident that all men are created equal.

"NO JUSTICE NO PEACE"

*N*one are so blind as those who will not see
*O*nly the righteous will ever "truly" be free
*J*ury's have the right to "recommend" life or death (but)
*U*nless the system is "just," it will destroy itself
*S*ome serving time because of the color of their skin
*T*rusting in a system "boasting" equality to "all" men
*I*ncarcerated because of a "Prejudicial Clause"
*C*aught up in a system of separate and unequal laws
*E*veryone's innocent until guilt is found
*N*otwithstanding this lack of justice the world around
*O*nly where there's harmony is there peace
*P*eople seeking it must face the beast (but if)
*E*ach one teach one, each one reach one
*A*ll willing to sacrifice until equality is won
*C*hallenging the system (as it is written) from within
*E*quality, Justice and Peace shall be ours to win.

Everyday, our world grows more complex. The challenge for a just and equal system is tested and retested, and tested again on a daily basis. For its foundation is based on the principle that each elected, appointed or empowered individual, adhere to their oath of office. And I truly believe that this will be a much better world for all men, for if we **know justice, we know peace.**

"Unless the system is 'just' it will destroy itself"

Many of us start off with a plan, a goal or a dream to strive for. But often times, we get off track, sidetracked or suffer setbacks. With our dreams and goals put on hold, they sometimes seem out of reach. And the day-to-day becomes a challenge of dealing with politics, policies and the sub-norm, leaving way for foolish shortcuts that seemingly, look inviting. Caught up in society's role by, situation or circumstance, often times leaves one feeling:

"HOPELESS"

A dream gone awry
Man caught-up in a vicious circle
Without the will to any longer try
Hope is that which was and seemingly is no more
Is no longer the reason (seemingly) to live for
A man tired of being a victim, a
Man caught up in society's role
Without a dream, a vision, or hope of reaching his goal
Fear no longer looms an "obstacle"

Be aware of two very important facts about going through the hardships of life. One, shortcuts or the easy way out, are very, very rarely as good as they seem. And two your situation usually isn't nearly as bad as it appears. Time heals, mends, restores and creates opportunities for new beginnings. It's written, **"this to shall pass."** Or, as they say in layman's terms, **"bad times don't last always."**

"A man without hope is a man without fear"

TRAIN UP
A CHILD
IN THE
WAY THEY
SHOULD GO

Way back, on the edge of another day and time, where respect was a given (until you violated the trust), obedience and expectation (because there was no such thing as child abuse), and children were children (when their parents were around), I remember:

"WHEN I WAS A CHILD"

When I was a child, I thought like a child, I Acted like a child
When my Parent's were around, but when they were gone, I acted
Like I was "grown."
When I was a child, I stayed in my place
When my parents were around, but when they were gone,
I stuck up my finger, licked out my tongue, shook
My "booty" and danced up a storm.
When I was a child, I said Yes Sir, No Sir.
And likewise with Ma'am, Excuse me, and Thank You.

As meek as a "Lamb" when my parents were around,
But when they were gone, I'd steal candy, I'd curse and
I'd sneak down the road, but atlas I'd get caught.
But atlas, I'd get caught and there would be dues to pay
For my father was a realist and he did not play.
And when he whipped my behind, reminding me I was but a
Child, he didn't whip any clothes and he lectured all the while.
And now when I think back to when I was a child, but a little older
And my parents weren't around, I thought like a child, I acted like a child,
I stayed in my place and kept a child's place, said Yes Sir and No Sir and
likewise
with "Ma'am," "Excuse me" and "Thank You" and was as meek as a Lamb.
I became a realist like my father, who taught it's the little things that help
To make "who" you are, and if you "earn" the respect of your elders
And peers in life, you'll go far.
Though you may never become what you
Choose to be in this society's role, at this point, may be unknown.
If you come to worship your God, know yourself and respect
your neighbors, you've succeeded, you're grown.
When I was a child, but now that I'm grown,
I put away my childish deeds.

It's been written, "Train up a child in the way (he or she) should go." The elders used to say, "bend a tree when it's yet a sapling and it will grow up straight and true." That went a long with, "go out there and get me a switch off of that tree," and "I thought I told you not to." Well, times have changed "for the better" they say, but I just can't remember so many young people being killed, going to jail or to prison. I can't remember so much disrespect to the elders, or blatant disrespect for the law (although in many cases it's hard to respect those who make the laws when those who make the laws break the laws). We need to check and often double check when our children are caught up and accused. Our young parents should know that, although society has set new guidelines in raising our children, if we don't teach them the basics or **"train up a child in the way they should go,"** then know that the **"rules change when they reach the age of accountability."**

"But Alas I'd Get Caught And There Would Be Dues To Pay"

Whether you were born with a gold card in your hand, a silver spoon in your mouth, or a dark cloud over your head, everybody has a story of how they got here from there. And most of us, if we let our minds sift through the times gone by, will find ourselves on occasion:

"BACK IN THE DAY"

Back in the day when I wore ragged

Clothes to school, wired shoes with cardboard soles

Back in the day when everything new was hand-me-down

Back in the day when we burned coal and had a pot belly stove (that

burned me)

Back in the day when we had to carry trees from the woods for heat

Chop it down, tote it up, cut it up and carry it in

All before getting ready for school

Back in the day when we didn't have indoor plumbing

And had to use the "outhouse"

Back in the day when I remember killing the rabbit

That provided all the meat we had for dinner

When corn meal was boiled and called a meal

Back in the day when my mother's children were hungry

And there was no food

I remember Fish Head Stew

Back in the day when we, as a family, picked all manner of fruit

Soaking in the morning dew - burning in the noonday sun

Back in the day when my father and mother actually fought

Their way through the stress and strain

Back in the day when a dose of caster oil was a cure all

When the only cure that my parents had for the hard times was

Alcohol

Back in the day when we got in trouble

Over the girls next door

The days when a "hard head" made for a "soft behind"

Back in the day, I never thought

That they would be the good ole days

Whether you call it memory lane, way back when, or a time gone by, every now and then,to remember how we got here from there, it's good to go **"back in the days."**

"Back in the days, when a dose of castor oil was a cure all"

It's been said that each generation sees things from a different perspective. Well, I'm from the "old school, the Baby Boomer Generation." And although that may be so, to some extent, can the seed, the leaf, the bud or the fruit, not acknowledge the branch, the trunk, the root, or "the seed?" (Cycle ending always beginning anew).

"THE OLD SCHOOL"

I'm from the "old school," yeah I've been around
But it wasn't long after I left that they tore it down
It's sad it had to fall, I seen it meet its final curtain call
Out with the old and in with the new
But it seems some of the rules fell with it too
Seems with it went some of the discipline and pride
In part that "can do" spirit that was taught inside
A movement, a cause, the cause seems to all but died
I come to you from a time gone by
That you might know the reason why

That if you're throwing your life away, you shouldn't act in haste
It's true - a mind's a terrible thing to waste
Sometimes the hardest thing to do is to listen for your own good
To your parents and teachers telling you do what you should
Well, maybe I can get you to listen to an old Soul Brother from the hood
For it's not about impressing your peers, getting high or getting laid
It's about getting educated then you're really getting paid
It's not about winning battles, for we win them everyday
It's about a debt you owe, for the many sacrifices by those
who've paved the way
It's about a responsibility that's handed down to you
That you should train up the next generation and bring them through
For, after awhile, it will be you, whom I hope
Will be heard to proudly say: "Yeah, I'm from the old school"
My class is world "renown"
It was "my generation"
Who turned it <u>ALL</u> around

Take a look around you and know that in every avenue of life, in every success and failure, in every advantage and disadvantage, in every opportunity, with every vote or political choice, and every take it for granted norm, there have been sacrifices, there have been those before you, me and us who've paved the way. And they've left a legacy for us to build on.

Now, take a look back at your family tree and see where you are (your linage, how you've branched out, are branching out, or budding, seeds, flowers, or new branches). Pass it on. It is or could be, or soon will be, up to you to make the tree strong.

"It's about a responsibility handed down to you"

Looking back over yesterday's gone by and filtering through that which has brought us to where we are today; I often reflect on how certain things are almost set in stone, stair steps to live and grow by: respect, education, and self-disciple and honor seems to be, at times, things that are lost to:

"THE WAY IT USED TO BE"

It used to be when a man brought children into
The world, he'd take care of his own
But nowadays you'd be truly pressed
To find a man in the home
It used to be that divorce was taboo, that when
You said for "better or worse" that's what you'd do
It used to be to have a child out of wedlock
Was a "disgrace" but nowadays it's commonplace
Hard to find shame on anyone's face,
Used to be that "respect" was a given,
Now it's truly something you have to earn
That "education" was a must (It yet is)
But it's a hard lesson for the last two generations to learn,
Used to be that parents and teachers would work together
Now it seems they are on opposite sides
No one seems to want to follow the rules
Even those who (make) the rules won't abide,
It used to be that a man was known by his word
And his "word" was his "bond"
But I guess the last two generations must have failed
To pass it on Father to Son

To take the best of what was and use it to better yourself, your people, your country and your world, then we are allowing the "wisdom of the ages" to be passed on to better the next generation, from generation to generation. Everyday is another challenge, to some it's a challenge just to make it to another day

"Pass it on father to son"

We are addressing a generation caught up in society's role, where the seeds of man, at a very young age, become subjected to many very harsh elements of society; those of an often unyielding street and or nightlife. We live in a society that builds more prisons than colleges. But surely, we play a part in this scenario, and must also answer to why:

"IT'S COME TO THIS"

It's come to this - little boys threatening the extinction of the bloodline
By getting themselves killed or doing hard time
It's come to this - little boys selling drugs, little girls "turned out"
Children having children, not knowing what life's all about
It's come to this - we're becoming a people in a vicious circle reverting to
the things of old. Because we don't read, don't listen, don't search or
seek, let the truth be told
It's come to this - we burn up a lot of negative energy on what is, what is
not, what could be, what should be and hanging out. Confused people,
with insane solutions who are ready to die ("Ha") for a cause they are not
ready to live for
It's come to this - Black on Black crimes at an all time high
Drive-by shootings where the innocent die, fighting and dying over the
color of the rag on your head; when you're all a different shade of black,
Whether your bandanna is blue, black, green, brown or red
It's come to this - the mothers of our ghettoes, inner cities
And mostly where there's drug-infested neighborhoods,
Have cried (and are crying) a river of tears
That runs parallel to a river of blood,
Shed by those in their younger years
It's come to this - where do we go from here?

Surely, all of us are not confused nor is the majority of our solutions insane, but the scene is played out for us daily. And surely we are not speaking of the majority, but the scene is played out to us daily. You don't have to acknowledge it, but you see it, you hear it, you read it, and you live it.

"Confused people with insane solutions who are ready to die (ha)
for a cause they are not ready to live for"

If you've tried to be a good parent and lead in the right way then it's a good thing when you can see your child adhere to your teaching. But it's often breathtaking when the event is totally unexpected, and it's at that point you can see:

"Something Within"

It wasn't verified and barely even questioned
But he was seemingly driven by something within
To orchestrate an explanation
But didn't seem to know quite where to begin
Something within him though wouldn't let him be
I could see it in his eyes as they flickered to the floor
and back to me
That little (big) boy aurora, at this moment, was all but gone
But I never expected him to confess to the unknown
For he boldly, yet humbly, stood there in his youth
Seemingly having summarized the possible consequences
He yet chose to reveal the truth
His eyes cast to the floor, rose like the rising sun
Connecting with my eyes he confessed to what he had done
He stood there in his youth anticipating what was to come
Seemingly content and relieved as though a battle had been won
I stood there overcome by the moment
Watching the man emerge from within my son

When you take a little love (a lot is recommended), praise, guidance and support and add a little of this and that you nurture, encourage and discipline your child. And once you've blended and added your love, nurturing, and support, as needed, you pray (continuously).

"Something within him though wouldn't let him be"

The seed of courage is planted at a moment's notice and often at a very young age. And sibling rivalry, peer pressure and the unknown test it. It's that untapped resource that makes heroes of mere men, leaders of lesser men, and overpowers the fear that destroys the dreams and visions of most men.

"IT TAKES COURAGE "

It takes courage to be a leader
To choose your own path and way
To not be led by others
Who could possibly lead you astray
It takes courage to go against the flow
When "everybody else is doing it"
To simply say "no"
It takes courage
To boldly stand your ground
When, to defend their point of view
Others will put you down
It takes courage
To stand against "peer pressure"
But don't let it ruin your plans
Remember you are responsible for your own actions
And the responsibility of your "Dreams and Goals"
Are, in part, held in your own hand.

Before you can become the master of your dreams and goals, you must first find the courage to face your fears. Become a leader of one if never of many. Dare to stand alone in the face of adversity, and have the courage to just say NO, to that which could separate you from your dreams and visions.

"It Takes Courage to go against the flow"

A ways back, on this walk of mine, my first born, Anita Shari, approached and faced this point of life. My efforts at this time, like so many other parents, were to somewhat give my blessings and turn over the reins. **(Whew! What a long haul. And yeah, you did it, "happy tears," a blessing, and to some, who wasn't sure they'd make it, a near miracle).** And when this time of year comes around, for you are now young adult, to wade out into the main stream of life, whether from the big city, suburbs, or small town, you might say as I did unto mine:

"YOU'RE OUT ON YOUR OWN"

You're out on your own now, starting a new
Your destiny is seemingly all up to you
It's up to you (now) which path you will choose
Or whether you will win with society's clues
Make mistakes, get involved, go to college or get a job
Join the service, see the world, or settle down
With your favorite guy or girl
Newfound freedom, you're out on your own
The whole world is your stage
And it's time to perform
You've been waiting for this day
It's finally arrived
The stage is set; the foundation has been laid,
You're even ready for a few mistakes to be made
Remember no man is an island
And you can't grow alone
Some decisions are made for you
It's a lot of responsibility of being grown
It's always good to have a plan
But remember the wise things your parents
And teachers have said
Don't set your goals out of reach
Nor let success go to your head
Don't burn down the bridges
That has brought you thus far
And where ever life takes you,
Be proud of where you came from,

And who you are
Remember that dreams take effort and commitment,
They don't just come to be
Keep that old school winning spirit. Don't be a quitter
For success can be found down avenues, you're yet to see
Beware the traps society has laid
That will steer you from the goals you've made
Go where you will, become what you must
With honesty, integrity, and with the prayers of all of us
And as you venture out into the unknown no matter how far
May the winds of time someday bring you back home?
To those who love you, for whom you are

This one's for the leaders of tomorrow. The whole world is your stage, just remember, we'll be watching. And as you go forward in whichever direction you choose, remember, **don't burn down the bridges, be proud of where you came from and who you are. Success can be found down avenues you've yet to see."**

"And may the winds of time someday bring you back home to those who love you for Who You Are"

It's a cycle always ending, and yet, beginning a new. Seeds are planted, flowers grow and bloom, and then comes the harvest and the reaper. But too many times, the reaper is premature, and the flower is harvested before its time.

"ABSTAIN"

Abstain refrain
Children having children
Gives you growing pains
Juggling a baby - school and or a job
Leads you down a road that's long and hard
Think you've got a man, proud and strong,
The exception to the rule, who'll take care of his own
But after the fact would truly be sad
To discover a two timing hustler or a deadbeat dad
His intentions were good, his words sincere
But commitment so young could cause great fear
The words he said blended with the night
The passion in his kiss, rhythm of the music
And the serenity of the light
Who could have known what one unprotected night
would bring
A passionate summers night, a baby in the spring
Abstain, Refrain, wait a while
Don't be another teenage mother with a fatherless child
It's a lot of hard work having a child of your own
But it's twice as hard trying to raise one "all" alone,
Abstain, Refrain - wait awhile
Don't be another teenage mother with a fatherless child.

And the seeds of time are again planted premature and the cycle ending, yet beginning, has once again begun. Well, this one's for all the young ladies, young women and girls. Beware, the reaper cometh, don't let beauty, being pretty, popular, or a plain Jane cause you to be victimized.

"Who could have known what one unprotected night would bring"
***
"Don't to be another teenage mother with a fatherless child"

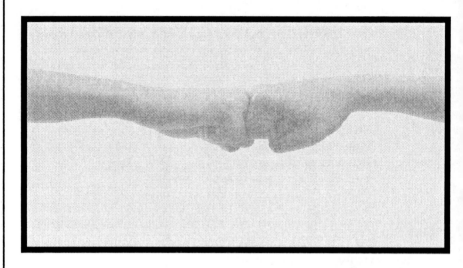

Now here is one of the heaviest, responsible, respected words in the world. To be a good Father is to train up a child in the way (he or she) should go. It's not just playing a part in bringing life, it's molding, shaping, helping, directing, disciplining, protecting and leading by example...

"FATHER"

Faithful in rearing the children
Attentive to their care
Treasuring the time that's shared together
Helpful in times of despair
Eager to express concern and praise
Righteously leading through Love, Discipline and Prayer

A good father is also responsible; he considers the needs of his child (or children). And does what he can to provide (or help provide), and the one thing that a father can do to help solidify his efforts in training is to live a righteous life and leading by example.

"Righteously leading through Love, Discipline, and Prayer"

We live in a day and age where East and West intertwine and the North and South co-exist with the flick of a switch or the push of a button. Where "fantasy" often seems a more rational choice of life, we many times submerge ourselves in a CD, DVD, VIDEO, ANTIMATED parallel world, universe or dimension. But no matter how far we go, or the extent of our circle, we eventually must face:

"REALITY"

Reality, it surges and splashes upon the banks of our fantasy
And often times washes upon our feet and connects us to that
Which we only read about or visualize from afar
It's ABC, NBC and CBS
It's CNN, MTV and BET
It's every time you turn on the news
It's what's highlighted in the critic's reviews
It's what the little children see everyday
It's factored into the games they play
It's video games, CD's and the Internet
It's a prophesy, a message, it's what we've come to expect
It's a warning, a precaution, a line drawn in the sand
It's life, it's death, it's man's inhumanity to man
It's an effort to enlighten, a distant negotiation
It's one man's release of his own frustration
It's the realization of another darkened dream
It's a cry, a plea, it's a scream....
Maybe you can't see it
Cause it doesn't directly affect you and it's not your concern - until it do
It's black, white, red, yellow, green and brown
The big city, Suburbs and the small town
It happens without warning
Without reason or rhyme
Makes you wish (sometimes) you were born
In another place and time
It's a dream, a cause, a vision of a new day
It's a remedy, a cure, it's the reality of Today

"Trying to open the eyes of the children of man before they are harvested by minds of destruction," has always been an unyielding passion of mine. And there have been many, many victims and battles lost, but the war rages on. And the reality of it all is that we set the stage.

We mark on, mark up, and mark dreams, goals, visions and the now by that which we allow to be accepted as legal and binding, socially acceptable, fashionable and, of course, politically correct. And, in doing so, we tarnish the seeds of tomorrow with diminished values of seeking political stature, risqué fashion statements, not training up a child in the way they should go. And by sitting back and allowing a justice system to become a "legal system" by which it is legal to market hate, corruption, nudity, satanic idolatry, and even killing our children on the games that our children play.

And then we wonder, after taking prayer out of the schools, why our children die at such an early age, why they are considered targets, why the cycle of violence seems to intensify yearly, and why more crimes demonstrate man's inhumanity to man.

But it's not really your concern because, for whatever reason, you're above or exempt from this reality. And if you can't wake up to this reality now, then remember it when it's your turn.

"It's what the little children see every day, it's factored into the games they play"

Often society sets traps to catch, let's just say, some of those who are considered the less scrupulous among us. Often our young people get caught up with those with such character, or try to represent, by exhibiting one with less scruples (caught up in society's role). And taking on a not so friendly, patience, or considerate world. Daring to go against the flow and walking head first into this great big wide wall-to-wall web with blinders on. It's a plan, a plot, a scheme, a trap. For most, always there's:

MORE THAN MEETS THE EYE

You think you can beat him at his own game (but)
Sometimes things aren't, as they appear to be
Think you can play the odds and win, maybe, maybe not
For some things are clearly made "clear" for you to fail
Yet, success can be found down avenues you're yet to see
But you must have Faith, Courage and Vision to prevail
Remember the warning signs, obtain and maintain self-control
Don't give up on your vision, your dreams, or your goal
Be "aware" of others "seemingly" in the same situation
Stay focused, though caught-up in "Society's Role"
Allow no one, to be harder on you then you are on yourself, (and)
When opportunity knock there's no telling what you'll find
For you'll yet be prepared, for chance,
When you learn to read between the lines
Because in life some things truly aren't as they appear to be.

Sometimes, the hardest thing in the world to see is that which is right before our eyes. For we are forever overlooking the obvious, because we so readily presume all things are as they appear to be. Well, here's one for your long-term memory; remember to remember there's usually More Than Meets The Eye.

For it's hard to beat a designed system in it's intent (just and observation, the prisons are full and as they build new ones (more so then colleges) they are soon filled.

"Stay focused, though caught up in "Society's Role""

It's a personal thing; it's all about your life, the quality of life, the responsibilities of life, your future, and maintaining the hard earned freedom of life. There are a lot of things that disrupts and corrupts the quality of life. The selling or the use of drugs is, unfortunately, a great concern in our society today. If we're defending the country like we're fighting the war on drugs, then we should all take up a foreign language, **because it was brought a long ways to be sold in the park.**

"SEE AND HEED"

I came before you with a plea
Don't tune me out before you hear what I have to say
Do you have dreams and goals and believe you're free
Drugs destroy dreams, put goals on hold, and make slaves of those that could be
Because drugs cause the bodies need to control the mind
I know that there are "pressures" that will make you not
Know which way to go
Who among you, think you know the way (Keep Living)
I wish I could come before you, having never been caught up in society's role
Am I to be as a voice crying in the wilderness, falling upon deaf ears
And are you going to be just another bad example for those in later years
Where do "we" begin to change what's come to be "be?"
I'm putting the burden of change mainly on you, but I'm
Going to let you know the key is right before your eyes
Praise is to be given to those who can "see and heed" prayer to
GOD that the effort is made and we all succeed.

And what about all the arrests and deaths that are associated with drugs and how detrimental is to the family structure? And you might wonder how such an advanced society can go so long without finding a better solution than legal slavery. Oh, you didn't know there's billion of dollars every year made off of the prison system.

Just remember that fulfilling dreams and goals is no meager task. And staying free from drugs, alcohol, and anything that incarcerates the mind, body or spirit, determines your ability to pursue or achieve your dreams and goals

"And are you going to be just another bad example for those in later years"

"I Don't Do Drugs Because I Know Who I Am And Where I Am Going Praise God"

Have you ever walked in the rain with something weighing heavily on your heart? Or searching for an answer to one of the many questions in life or while feeling the pain of a loved one lost? Did you notice, at times, how you couldn't tell whether you were crying or the heavens were crying for you?

"SO MANY TEARS"

**It's raining I've seen it this way before
On occasions when things were really bad
The rain takes on an odd feeling
It falls like tear drops on my face
The Angels are crying, another child is dying
Another going bad, another heart's being broken
Another mother's sad. Another boy becomes a
Man, but only by an intimate ritual is he bound
Children having children is now world renown
The Angels are crying So many tears
This generation must face so many fears
From bigotry to gang violence to pressure from
Their peers, Aids, drugs, unemployment, a wavering recession
Homelessness, welfare cuts, a state of depression
Our children are dying --- The Angels are crying
So many tears**

The pressures within this generation cause many to become caught up in "society's role" and many others to suffer their pain. The time of weeping is often upon us more than we'd care to admit. It makes us wonder if we're walking in the rainy season for our children. I think back when it was said, **"When a child dies, the Angels cry."**

"The Angels are crying, another child is dying"

Starting off with a plan, a goal, and having direction is essential for the road to success. But, every now and then, our plans fail or we fall short of our goals and in doing so, we often lose our direction. That's not always all bad because every day is another test of time, and we learn how to endure setbacks and to think outside of the box. But sometimes we get lost in the crossroads of life and find ourselves:

"CORNERED"

Standing on the corner shucking and jiving
Rapping and crooning, punching and jabbing, and hanging out
Sharing a bottle, sharing a lie
Viewing a scene from the inside-out
Echoing sounds that continue to make you question
Why am I out here on this corner
Not paying attention, caught up in the moment
Until a horn blows
And you wave at someone you know, or used to know
Passing by the corner catching your show
Out on the corner with your dreams and goals put on hold
Feeling a little embarrassed, a little ashamed

Caught up in society's role
It's times like these that make you remember when
And there you are standing at a crossroad again
With your dreams and goals off course and in need of repair
Questioning how you got here from there
Out of step with what used to be
Your dreams, goals, and being more in touch with reality
Not just going along with the flow or fitting in
But striving against the odds to win
Suffering many setbacks before this last one
But always managing to work it out and get it done
Realizing it's nothing like it should have been
But the hanging got easier and you started to blend
Never believing you'd do all you've done just to get paid
But like when you were a kid the principles of life you disobeyed
Started taking shortcuts to try to make up ground
But they turned out to be the long way home, the long way around
You know the way back and it's not by being a blood donor
The first step is to put   between you   and the corner.

If you can still question why you are on the corner. You can yet find the road to get you off. For there are those who have lost their way and those who are truly cornered. But you who question have avenues of hope.

"Not just going along with the flow or fitting in…. but striving against the odds to win"

So many young brothers believe they can beat the system. Some do, but the prisons are filled and overfilled with many who've been caught up in "society's role" (doing the expected). Denied their freedom and left only to ponder the fulfillment of their dreams and goals while they endure:

"Hard Times"

The gang violence and over all youth violence has become a disgrace
Black on Black crime is at an all time high
It's hard to just sit back and watch as our young brothers' die
It's hard to watch, as they become legal slaves
Even harder to watch as they're laid down in early graves
It's hardest yet to watch as the innocent die
Because our young brothers are so caught up in Society's Role
They execute the dreaded drive-by
Between the ages of fifteen and nineteen
Is where we're experiencing the most of our serious Juvenile crime
It's also between the ages of fifteen and nineteen
We find the most Juveniles who are locked up in their prime
It used to be you could do a crime
And not worry about doing hard time
You could get in and out of the system in but a little while
Because you were a teenager, a Juvenile
But the system is leaning toward holding juveniles responsible for their crim
In other words what they're saying is if you do the crime, you do the time
It should make no difference about your age
Is what the victims and their families rage
If you're old enough to do the crime, you do the time
Hard time, locked up in a cage

The suffering by the victims and their families and the anguish coupled with embarrassment and shame suffered by the accused family and the injuries and laying to rest of the innocent for just being in the wrong place at the wrong time. The agony and frustration of this is that in some places, it's the unfortunate norm. (No excuse is acceptable) But there are many reasons that leave us with a predator who at times is a victim (of society's role).

"It should make no difference about your age, is what the victims and their families rage"

Are you a part of the next generation? Well, if so, there is a bad rumor going around about the young men of your generation. It's being said that you are the gotta-have it now, will take a shortcut, somebody owes me something and I don't care because I will go out in a blaze of glory generation. We know that it's only a few bad apples. But they get all the press. Here's a little somethin' somethin' to think about for those few bad apples that's making some people cross the street just because:

"LITTLE BROTHER"

The world don't owe you anything
And only a few things are guaranteed
If you don't have what you want
Be thankful, if you have what you need
The easy way isn't always the best
There's no telling where it'll lead
Hard work and foresight, is the best
Way to succeed
Don't burn down your bridges
If you should make it across
And if you should err along the way
It's rarely ever a total loss
No man is an island
Be thankful for each and everyday
Don't ever get too proud, to bow down and pray
You should count your blessings
Don't be anyone's fool
Strive for wisdom and understanding
To be the Exception to the Rule

Everyone can't start at the top. And success is something you usually strive for. It takes patience, persistence and time. Success builds character and often teaches teamwork and appreciation. Focus beyond what's expected of you because someone else wrote a script and expects you to star in it. The only problem you're really having is adjusting to being in control of your own self worth and finding your direction and distancing yourself from those real non-conformists which don't have a dream or goal to pursue.

"And if you should err along the way, it's rarely ever a total loss"

The regularity of being caught up in the streets in some communities is like church on Sundays. The difference being is that the streets take in more than all the churches combined. For the gates to the streets are open everyday and everyday in that respect is Sunday. Whether being caught-up voluntary because of being caught up in "society's role" or involuntary because their parents or guardians are. Many parents are asking the questions...

"IS THAT MY CHILD? WHERE'S MY CHILD?"

He's a victim of society, caught up in society's role
He's a wayward child, because of circumstance
Alone in this great big world
With very little choice
Let's say a little prayer, for all the boys and girls
Who are forced out, into this cold, cold world.
Not because they're disobedient or bad
But because society got a choke hold on their Mom and Dad
Alcohol, Dope, Crack Cocaine just to experience the
High that will never ever change.
That will take you up for sure, but will bring you lower
Than you ever were before
Little boy running the streets, can't get a job
Got to steal to eat, he's a wayward child
Because of circumstance, a victim of society
With very little chance
Who's the blame, could it partly be you and I
We see it going on and stand idly by.
Is He A Victim?

After a while, in some cases, it becomes a question of is it them or us? Yet, think of your child or a child you know, becoming one of those wayward children. Is there anything you can do, or could have done to make a difference? Remember one of the old unwritten laws of the past, "It takes a whole village to raise a child."

"He's a victim of society, caught up in society's role"

The lure of the nightlife. Many are drawn by the sounds, the lights, and the ability to blend into the darkness. But often times, so many fall prey to the hypnotic, erratic, I can get away with it because it's dark, pace of the night, and are victimized by its always ever drawing undercurrent.

"Little Joe Cool"

You know the scene
A body lying beside the street,
Teenage boy beneath the sheet
Remember when he was younger - was angry
When told he couldn't go out to play
Got a little older, decided to "disobey"
Got caught up in the ways of the night
QUICK money, new friends, and a secret life
Not knowing what's done in the darkness comes to light
Who was this young man?
Let's call him, "Little Joe Cool"
From a single parent family,
Doing bad in school
Not because he couldn't do better
Or to stubborn to try,
But because his posse would tease him and ask him why
Saying you were born in the hood,
Raised in the hood and in the hood you will die
Little Joe Cool was an average Joe
Got caught up with or in the wrong crowd
And they wouldn't let go
It was their way or no way, he was too blind to see
It could cost his life just to get free
Little Joe Cool met Little Willie.
Now Little Willie was raw
He had death and destruction in his bag
And he adhered to Street Law
It's a buyers and sellers market
To Little Willie, to sale was to advance
Little Joe Cool bought but once
He didn't get a second chance

Good advice is only as good as it's received. And being a novice in the game of life subjects one to life's harsh realities. Sometimes, the harsh reality of life is death. So, it's not always good to be a follower. I encourage you to at least be a leader of one's self, and good advice is good advice, no matter where it comes from.

"He didn't get a second chance"

With each passing day, the tally fluctuates yet never seeming to go down. No longer is it just figures or names without faces. No longer is it mainly limited to the big city or gang related. For now, it's also in your town, your neighborhood and mine. The names and faces are familiar, even family, and they're caught up in that fluctuating tally and have all become statistics.

"STATS"

Another drive-by
Another young brother dying
Another **Black-on-Black** crime
Another Mother crying
Another young Brother lying in a heap
Fighting for his life
Against a new code of the streets
Another mugging in the park
Another **"CHILD OF GOD"** lost in the dark
Another young Brother facing a life of crime
Another statistic falling in line
Another prison society must build
Another grave for a young body to fill
Another hope for tomorrow gone
Another chance for the "Cause" blown
Another "Child" caught in the crossfire
Innocent blood is shed
Another **MARTIN, MALCOLM OR MANDELA,**
Lay dying or dead
Another gun, and another child has combined
To create horror in the night, we used to die for a cause,
But drugs and society's role, has distorted our plight
Now we're dying just because, and surely losing the fight
Children feeding on crack cocaine
Like Decon being fed to Rats
It's as though we can't see what's going on
"Blind as bats"
How do we stop it, this frenzied need
How can we salvage the sown and unsown seed
How do we open the eyes of the "teen-aged" Black Man
And convey to him **"HE MUST UNDERSTAND"**

He's caught in the web of the "unspoken plan"
Gym shoes, starter jackets, carjacks and jacks
Add to the statistic of **"BLACKS KILLING BLACKS"**

Now, there's a cornucopia of reasons to draw a line in the sand or barricade the hood to stop the free flowing flood of drugs and illegal guns. As surely as the struggle is real in the hood, the true struggle goes beyond our own meager boundaries and challenges us to make a positive difference. And if you don't appreciate the way things are, and are not a part of trying to find the solution, then you are a part of the problem. Cause - Cause - Cause - but not just because.

"And another Martin, Malcolm, or Mandela lay dying or dead"

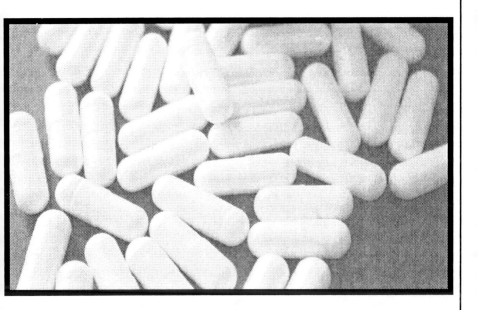

Grew up in a time where it was seemingly used as an antidote, all the pressures, stress and strain of just trying to cope with the every day norm. A time when alcohol was more so the drug of choice, a time when it seemed like nearly everyone had a gun. And I can remember the first time that I heard of marijuana. When the man across the street got busted for growing it between the rows of corn (it took me a few more years to realize his wife wasn't really half crazy most of the time.)

And now these three (drugs, guns, and alcohol) are etched into the fiber of our society, overpowering young and old, black and white, the rich and the poor. They've joined forces on a regular basis to try and steal the headlines in the newspapers and the six o'clock news.

"DRUGS, GUNS, AND ALCOHOL"

It's elaborate and it's cloaked
But it's well defined
It's on your street, in your neighborhood and mine
It's in your school; on you job, and even goes to church with you
It clouds attention, rational, and even point of view
It's no accident that it constantly stares you in the face
It's put there by intentional means to keep you in your place

It's drugs, guns and alcohol
It's a plan, a plot, a scheme
It's a conspiracy against your hopes, your goals and your dreams
It's on every other street corner, in the alley, and somewhere in the dark
It was brought a long distance to be sold in the park
It's guzzled, it's snorted, it's smoked, and semi-automatically fired
It's legal, illegal and by certain elements of society, it's admired
It's liquor, it's grass, it's powder, and it's all kinds of pills
It's regulated by someone in a suit and tie, and mandated by bills
It's above board, underground, black marketed, and even government sealed
And by boozing it, using it and oozing it, our young people are being killed
It destroys the family structure and removes the head of the household
It leaves the children and teenagers in a sub-jungle, running out of control
It's the reason why, the question why, mothers cry and the innocent die
It's that which fills our bellies with gall
It's Drugs, Guns and Alcohol

We all make choices, and if we learn to really consider the consequences of our actions, and the price of failure. And some things in life are set up for us to fail. And if you'll just remember that it's a conspiracy against your hopes, your goals and your dreams, and then you won't be so subjected to getting caught up in "society's role."

"It's put there by intentional means to keep you in your place"
***
"It's above board, underground, black marketed and even government sealed"

Seems like the Death Angel has taken up residence in the hood and his target is the seeds of man. The drugs, guns and alcohol, combined with that, often low self-esteem. Got less, need mo, bad role models (sporting the Bling-Bling), the fear of being perceived as less then, or being punked out, and all this combining to wedge them in the clutches of "society's role."

"THERE ARE NO CHILDREN HERE"

Born in the ghetto, free of vision
Lost in the maze of indecision
Can't see beyond the norm of things
Drugs, stray bullets, and darken dreams
There are no children here
They were all caught up in society's role
Gave up their youth for rocks, Uzi's, and chains of gold
Used to see them playing hoops down in the park
But now, because of the drive-by's
They only come out in the shadows after dark
There are no children here
They die or are incarcerated
Because of a genocide type mentality
Caught up in society's role, side-tracked
From the cause and their own reality
There are no children here
The seeds die before they can take root
Some by the high caliber of lead in the air
Others rap themselves around a rock
Which is not the solid rock and follow suit
Rocks, lead, and iron bars, are poor soils from which to grow
Yet caught up in society's role
Beyond this plot, there isn't much that they know
Born in the ghetto, rarely or never venturing out
Mind filled with wonder, self-esteem filled with doubt
There are no children here
Yet many seeds to be cast, row by row by row by row
We must cultivate, till, and refine the ground
For we reap that which we sow

Now, there's a shadow that's cast on many, in many walks of life, (it's really void of race or color). And is as far reaching as the East is from the

West makes you wonder if the children are living by example. For they can't see their way beyond their turf wars, drug infested hoods, alcohol on nearly every corner, and the peer pressure from many of their efforts to separate themselves from the rat race.

Some to the degree of having those fifteen minutes of fame mentality (or what someone outside the hood would say, "having that ghetto mentality") coincide with adulthood and our white, blue and no collar efforts to climb the social ladder, or maintain our so-called social statuesque.

"They die or are incarcerated by a genocides type mentality"

There are many drugs out there that are detrimental to your dreams, goals and health. But only a few are more vicious than the demon crack cocaine. Its affordability (from the start), and accessibility are pluses to make it your drug of choice. But know it desires to be not just your drug of choice, but your only choice. For there are those who have chosen to live just for it, and there are those who make choices and die for it. There are those who choose to "addict" others for it; family, friends, strangers and even children. We make choices everyday; choose to walk away, run away, refuse it, turn it down, or even just say no. Get angry if someone approaches you about it. (Seek help for them.) Flee from it while you have the choice. Remember, there are only a few drugs more vicious than "the demon"....

"Crack Cocaine"

Caught in the web, yet
Running for his life
Always looking over his shoulders
Cause of the lifestyle, of his addiction
Kicked in the "gonads" by the agony of his affliction
"CRACK"
Children, "yes children," caught up in the system pawns in the game of death
Out of touch with reality, "Slaves within themselves"
Caught up, strung out, addicted to the need
Against all odds how can they succeed?
Infiltrated by the blight that destroys self
Nobodies "friend" a product of white death,
Eroding a society from within. Nobody's friend, nobody's friend
"COCAINE"

We make choices everyday; choose to walk away, run away, refuse it, turn it down, casually pass, boldly retort, or even just say no, while you have a choice, use it wisely.

"Infiltrated by the blight that destroys self"

Charles Edward Peterson, SR.

Have you ever been wrong? Not just, ok so what's wrong, but you're going to have to pay the price wrong. At any time have you ever bitten off more than you could chew, or grabbed hold to more than you could handle. Have you ever took on a dare, or went along just because everybody else was doing it, maybe or maybe not. But surely temptation has crossed your path somewhere along your way. Maybe you don't believe the decisions you made have any merit on how you got here from there, but then, maybe it made all the difference in your world.

"LOOKING BACK"

Flipping, turning, filtering, scanning, searching
Trying to find a time when you were in control
Control of your own destiny or just in control
A time when dreams were dreams
Not nightmares running amuck in reality
A time when there really was a light
At the end of the tunnel
A time when, at least, you knew there was a tunnel
A time when hope was something worth believing
A time when there was raising and falling
But yet, at least, breaking even
Back, back, back, beyond the now
Beyond the this can't be happening
Beyond the how did I get here from there
Back beyond the maybe, maybe, somebody else,
"but not me"
Back, back unto a time when at least it was done
Under the cover of darkness
Beyond the afflicted, restricted and convicted
Beyond the time when reality conflicted
With the realization of being addicted
Back beyond the last time, the first time
When you had the foolish notion
You were stronger then the demon potion
Back beyond the rock, which was not the solid rock
Where you chose the broad road, instead of the narrow path
Where you didn't just say no

Back, back beyond the "aw, it'll be alright"
It shouldn't hurt to try it "just" once (Repeat)
It's only a half a hit, only a half a hit
Looking back, looking back, looking back
Beyond that first, undeniable urge "t o d o i t a g a i n."

Don't ever believe you're that strong, or ever get that stressed out, or go along with the flow to that degree just to fit in. It won't solve the problem, make it alright for a while, or give you class. And once the spirit of the drug is in you, you become the host.

"When you had the foolish notion you were stronger then the demon potion"

CIRCLES

Around and around and around we go, where we're going to stop at, most people don't even know. How to get back to the straight and narrow, how to stop this insatiable, revolving cycle that has become life. This spinning, somewhat out of body experience that often leaves one in a whirlwind of wonder, that keeps us going in:

"CIRCLES"

I keep going around in circles
And the answers I can't find
And I've also got a half-a-million questions
All locked up in my mind
I keep going around in circles
Around and around all the time
Looking for the answers
To the questions on my mind
The world keeps going in circles
And millions of problems can't be solved
People seem to make their own problems
By getting or not getting involved
Spinning wheel, spinning all the time
Like an oasis in a thirsty man's mind
A mind as deep as an ocean of sand
Sifting through an "hour glass"
Half sand, half man
Circles, circles, circles, out of one circle
Into another, but keeping in mind the memory of the other
Got caught up answering the questions
Questioning the answers
Always in doubt
But came up finally with a solid answer

That was so simple I wanted to shout
A new beginning, a new beginning is the only way out

If you find yourself, meeting yourself, chalk it up to trying to find yourself. And if you should ever get that mid-day, mid-way, mid-life, hourglass, half sand, half-man feeling, then look up for a new beginning.

"Got caught up answering the questions, questioning the answers"
***
"A new beginning is the only way out"

Everyone has a story. Some stories stems from the highest branch of its family tree to its very roots. And with each story, comes a reason and cause. Yet, each having or playing a part in the make up of how we got here from there. And surely those who taught us valuable lessons expected us to use it for our betterment and to pass the ones on that could help others, through the changing of time.

"CHILDREN OF THE PAST"

If we take of the knowledge
We learned of yesterday gone by, we
Can't allow those same old excuses to
Go on that has prevented many of us from going
Forward excuses that have become a way of life
With many of us daring not to
Open the clinched fist helping to confuse the
Minds of this generation and surely the generations to come
Then and now is a different time and place
We'll always remember and should teach our children
Forever isn't too long to relate how we got "here" from "there" but to
Remain in the web of hate and anger is to be as
Children neither responsible nor concerned
Of the degradation of self, nor the doors that are opened
The present acknowledge the lessons of the
Past and lays the foundation for the future

Revealing if we're always looking back for cause and excuses, we may not see the doors of opportunity open before us. Surely, and truly, many see and believe there to be an unbalance to the scales of justice.

"Forever isn't too long to relate how we got here from there"
***
"BUT IF WE CAN'T GO FORWARD WITH OPEN MINDS;
THEN WE'LL FOREVER REMAIN CHILDREN OF THE PAST"

The eyes of the world are upon us. The light at the end of the tunnel is surely illuminated. For, I can see it through the cracks in the door of opportunity. So why are some of us still going through the backdoor? Is it because the avenues are often cluttered with detouring obstacles? Didn't you know that there was a major effort made to get the doors of opportunities opened and it's going to take the same kind of effort to keep it open and open it wider for this and generations to come:

"THE SEEDS OF MAN (A HERITAGE TO RECLAIM)"

Where you say gang
I say tribe
Where you say die
I say survive
Where you say "I don't care because"
I say too many have died for the cause
I say you focus too much on the past
Instead of the problems at hand
We are the richest bloodline on earth
We're the seeds of man
We have a heritage to reclaim
It should be done in our Fathers' name
Done with humility, pride and not shame for
To reflect what is before us is to become but the same
Our task is the beast to tame
Turn the hunter into the game
Not to destroy, but to change
So that mankind may endure
That our SOULS may be saved and made pure
For the greater task we were put here for
To find for hate a cure

Prejudice, bigotry, and any other form of hatred is not something that is inherent; it's more often is fueled by a fire of ignorance and fear and it's going to take a whole lot of patience and prayer.

"To reflect what is before us is to become but the same"

Generation upon generation have stood still and watched as their spiritual and moral values have been eroded right before their eyes. Now, we are in an era of children having children in single parent homes. A new standard of discipline set by law. An era where respect is no longer given and where value of life is often deemed as less valuable then the clothes on your back. We live in an era where teenagers are subjected to the harshest realities of life and the law because, at times, they are caught up in "society's role."

But all is not lost. For as surely as we have advanced in many areas and era of the degradation of principles and values, we are also blessed to be in:

"THE GENERATION OF CHANGE"

Where did it all begin?
Do we have any idea where it's going to end?
We must make preparations to start anew
Begin the beginning of the end of what we're going through
To regain a hold on that which is out of control
Change the attitudes of those who've lost sight of their dreams and goals
That new "role models" can be planted like seeds
Which will instill dignity, respect and pride which
Has all but blended into the darkness and died
Come with a new attitude, reasoning and hope
To help alleviate the drive-bys, children having children, and the dope
Be not the generation of statistics, but the generation of change.

The legacy of life was given to us through trial and error that we might overcome the negative influences of the power of the air. We must overcome, not become clones of that which was before us. It is our responsibility to pause for the cause, rationalize and recognize, and reflect and visualize. And by doing so we will see just how far we've come and how far we've drifted from the old landmarks. We must begin to accept responsibility for the parts we have played in our own demise or change.

"Where do we begin to change that which has come to be?"

The baton has been passed and we've been handed the responsibility to carry the vision, the dream and the cause. Actually, it would seem that we are in a very opportune time in life. Blessed with the common sense and grit of our forefathers, the legacy of the cause and struggle woven through our every success and failure, and the natural awareness of the need and urgency of the now. We are armed with the wisdom and understanding that violence begets violence and that our paths are directed within the bounds of a defined system.

And through the process of time, trial and error, we have been harshly educated that the system is not a justice system but a legal system. So, with all the avenues of understanding before us, it behooves us to work within the bounds of the system to make the system work. The system is designed for the good of the people and the country and not for frailties of the human factor which would indeed be the optimum system of life (or close to it).

But if the system fails you (or your people), you have the inherent right (legally at any given time) within the system to voice your disapproval.

"IF NOT US WHO (IF NOT NOW WHEN)"

If we as a people are to ever achieve equal voice
Not be subjected or forced avenues of choice
Us against them is not the way to succeed
Who will stand, with reason, and take the lead
If we can't somehow learn how to close the gap today
Not just us but our children, and children's children will pay
Now is the time for wisdom, understanding and reason to prevail
When we learn the urgency of now, and stand as one, we shall not fail

It's no longer acceptable to allow the system to go along unchecked (or in the hands of those who may not have your best interest within the bounds of the law at heart). That's another reason why we should "train up a child in the way they should go that they may rightly divide the word of truth."

"Now is the time for wisdom, understanding and reason to prevail"

What if the world were engulfed in darkness and all we could see was shadows. Or the light was so bright that all was void of color. What would it be then that would prejudice the spirit of man?

There isn't, in many ways, anything wrong with seeking to gain an advantage. But there are some things in life we should acknowledge that we share equally.

"WHAT WILL IT TAKE"

There are short ones, tall ones
Big ones, small ones
Dark ones, light ones, black ones, white ones
And all the beautiful shades in between
There are smart ones and those not so smart
Those with character, those with heart
Those with pride and hindsight
Those who'll do the right thing, simply because it's right
Those holding onto a dream which will never die
Those afraid of failure, but not so too afraid to try
Those who have their heads on straight and are on a mission
Those who remember the dream and have a vision
Those caught up in society's role
Blind with anger and out of control
Those who manipulate the system from within
Destroying life with the stroke of a pen
Those who sit in judgment of other men
Just because of the color of their skin
Who won't see you as an individual (responsible for all you do)
But hold the majority accountable for the deeds of a few.
What will it take for us to become as one
Can the "seeds of man" unite after all that's been done?
Will it take an "invasion" from outer space
Or the "Second Coming" to unite the human race

Well here is one for the history books. We've surely (as the folks we're fastly becoming used to say), "got a long row to hoe". But if we don't try to change it today, then our children, and children's children, will have to pay.

"Can the *Seeds of Man* unite after all that's been done"

It was like something only believed possible in fiction. But the truth is our mighty shores could not protect us from an enemy within from another horrid act of man's inhumanity to men. For the war of the world finally struck home. And as you look upon, reflect upon, and sadly grieve for those lost (be they loved ones or strangers), let this be a day of prayer and national remembrance. But as I look back over many of man's other atrocities, trying to love my enemy as I do myself, about this inhumane event, I can't help but wonder:

"I Wonder...(911)"

I wonder if they knew if it ever came to mind
If they ever even imagined what would happen
To those they left behind,
I wonder if they could have seen
The chain reaction that would take place,
Would they have been so willing
To stare death in the face,
Or would they have been willing to reevaluate

Possibly even try to negotiate,
Was there one who could have came forward to mediate
To curve the horrible chain of events on that unforgettable date,
Would they have been willing to sacrifice
The lives of so many of their own
If they could have looked into the future
If they had but known,
Would they have been willing
To carry out such a bold and dastardly plan
That will go down in history
High on the list of man's inhumanity to man,
Would they have forsaken this terrible thing they done
And spared the lives taken (since and) on 911.

As more and more of our hometown troops risk and lose their lives in the aftermath of this calamity, I can't help but look back and wonder what would cause such hatred in the hearts and minds of those who took many lives and who would give up their natural lives for their cause.

What a tragedy, but unless the powers that be truly return to following a higher power, we shall continue to wonder....

"If they could have looked into the future, if they had but known"

Patriotism is more than a notion when you are often in the midst of those who don't hold its true virtue (moral excellence, goodness, righteousness), essence (the basic real and invariable nature of a thing), or significance (the quality of having a special meaning) to that worthy standard. A true patriot stands up for the greater cause to defend the principle of the foundation. And if you harm, misuse, or leave behind the least of those excepted as a part of the whole, then the patriot in patriotism has become as a "rebel without a cause." Brandishing the banner of a false allegiance and adding to the degradation of a deteriorating principle.

Just as those who ask for, when in need, and give not when able...

"ASK NOT"

Ask this generation and they can't remember the assassination of JFK
Not so in my mind, I yet remember that ill-fated day
What a miscarriage of justice our nation did receive
Your rights and mine given the heave
Country torn asunder, the beliefs of an elected official causes death
Can we ever blot out this stain that this tragedy left
Do the love of country deserve such an end
For what better reason to live than God country and peace among men
You and I can learn a lesson from histories review
But you must believe in God and country and do what you have to do
What can we do to help lead our country to one nation under God?
You and I must find a way to not always live by the rod
Can we make this country better, seemingly one of JFK's dreams?
Do we leave it to others as often it seems
For it's everyone's responsibility in this melting pot
Your opinion and mine may differ, but our rights certainly not
Country of many nations, we've become, rights of the many, protects rights
of the one

Surely our country and all the elements that make up its basic principle of life is a worthy cause if the moral fiber of its bill of rights hinges on and truly supports equal rights.

"Your opinion and mind may differ, but our rights certainly not"

There are those among us who are worthy of acknowledgement because of the good deeds they've done for humanity, some in their chosen field of study, and others by their heroic efforts and stands. One such man boxed his way to legendary status, with poetry and prophecy, backed up by The Ali Shuffle, and a magnum of combinations and flurries (and later, the rope-a-dope). He stuck his fist in the ground and turned the world around.

And then Ali done the unexpected for some, and the only thing he could do in the eyes of others, he refused to play in the game of war. Refused to step forward and be drafted, upholding his God, his religion, and stood on his principle of not taking another human life (if you don't know the rest of the story, check it out at the library, DVD's, or boxing Heavy Weights).
A living legend, and now an **"Ambassador of Peace."**

"A L I"

Float, float, float with speed, power and form
Like a leaf in harmony with the eye of the storm
A legend carving notches in the rings of time
Butterfly, shuffling, spouting prophecy and rhyme
Sting, sting, sting with wisdom, balance and grace
Like a great thoroughbred setting the pace
A Gatling gun spitting fire the ultimate repeater
Bee made honey, couldn't be sweeter
Rumble young man, rumble
Your real life super hero in and out of the ring
Hands, hands, hands so quick, flurrying punches unseen
Can't match the rhythm that's unique
Hit with combinations that's oh so sweet
What he also done was used rope-a-dope -- give his people hope
Your champ and mine, the people's champ could cope
Eyes of the dragon, swift of hand, feet and mind
Can't be equaled through the annals of time
See, there are many champions, champs to be; but the Greatest yet is

Muhammad Ali

Where do these warriors come from? Surely they don't always fit the mold that we would categorize todayas **leaders, heroes, and nowadays role models**. They may be the exception to the rule in their chosen field, or gifted to the degree of eclipsing most any adversary or opponent, and they're often considered legendary within their own life times. These individuals usually always became bigger than their chosen profession (some didn't even have professions, they saw a need and sought to fulfill it) to the degree that whatever it is (or was), that they excelled in it and it overflowed into the mainstream differences and issues of society. You know like Dr. King, Sojourner Truth, Abe Lincoln, Jesse Owens, Joe Lewis, J.F. Kennedy's, Booker T. Washington's, Betsy Ross's, Harriet Tubman, Malcolm X's, Frank Robinson's, W.E.B. DuBois and many others unnamed, unknown yet forever remembered for their contributions to a better society.

"Float like a butterfly, sting like a bee, your hands can't hit what your eyes can't see"

PART III

Charles Edward Peterson, SR.

DREAM

That Transcends

"When I care to be powerful--to use my strength in the service of my vision--then it becomes less and less important whether I am afraid."
Audre Lorde

CHASING AFTER A DREAM

In the midst of finding ourselves, plotting our course, and weeding out fantasy from our reality, we are blessed with dreams, and often visions of a better day. We strive to enhance the quality of life, develop character, personality, and establish some degree of stability. And even though we may find a measure of success in our effort, we come to realize that "reality" is often very stressful.

On the one hand, a worthy dream can punctuate the quality of life, create avenues of escape from the norm, and often give life fulfillment.

*But, there are many things in the realm of reality that we certainly must strive for. Like believing in ourselves; that **The Finished Effort** will be better; in preparing ourselves for **OPPORTUNITY** before it knocks; and even in striving to do **A GOOD DEED**.*

*There is always time for dreams, but sometimes dreams should be put on hold, as also that desire which is your goal. But, if you're blessed to face **ANOTHER TEST OF TIME**, and it doesn't illuminate the light at the end of the tunnel, then you might want to focus in on **THE AMERICAN DREAM** (for a dream come true would be such **A SWEET SAVOR**). Or remember that, fantasy in reality is a natural part of you, and that worthy **DREAM**" in our lives help stop us from **SERVING TIME** and are but a different perspective.*

*So, let us prescribe a little **MEDITATION PROCLAMATION** as we strive to maintain our daily dose of reality while **CHASING AFTER A DREAM**.*

Charles Edward Peterson, SR.

CHASING AFTER A DREAM

DREAMS

THE AMERICAN DREAM

THE FINISHED EFFORT

CHASING AFTER A DREAM

MEDITATION PROCLAMATION

OPPORTUNITY

A SWEET SAVOR

A GOOD DEED

ANOTHER TEST OF TIME

SERVING TIME

Sometimes, too much talking gets in the way of what needs to be said, but it's not often that a few words are able to define the totality of a subject. That being the case, behold what it takes to make a Dream come true.

"DREAMS"

Dreams take commitment, effort and time
Patience and persistence, like mountains to climb
Dreams take a desire above the norm
One must sometimes be driven, as in a raging storm
Yet, Dreams must sometimes be put on hold
As also, that desire which is your goal
For sometimes in life, one must refrain
    (From being a Dreamer)
For the present reality to sustain

Well, if that's not a road map, it's an **Advance to Boardwalk** (when it's for sale and you can afford it, and you already own **Park Place),** and you can put up hotels, and all the other players are about rounding the corner at **Free Parking**), **and if you pass go collect**... The only difference being, you can advance in reality. For now, you know just what it takes to make your dream a reality. And it's not procrastination, slackness, or lack of quality time...

"DREAMS TAKE EFFORT, COMMITTMENT, AND TIME"
***
(AND DON'T FORGET THE PATIENCE AND PERSISTENCE)

Whether in the depths of our subconscious, in an envious eye, or on the tips of our tongue, *The American Dream* plays a part in the lives of many of us. And sometimes in this fast food, fast lane, gotta-have it now generation, the patience to achieve it is often the weakest link in the chain.

"THE AMERICAN DREAM"

Its beach front condos and sandy shores
High-rise apartments with revolving doors
Its planes, trains and limousines
Rubbing elbows with "Kings and Queens"
No more living from check to check
When you speak, you're getting respect
No more fast foods – it's rare cuisine
The Jet Set, the fast lane, living large
A fantasy house with an eight-car garage
It's a helicopter pad on a big estate
A beautiful garden and an electric gate
It's success and opportunity well in hand
The inside track and a working plan
No longer a bench player on the corporate team
A self-made *reacher* of "The American Dream"
No more striving to reach the grade
Blessed beyond measure, all debts are paid
Yet counting my blessings each and every day
Remembering where I came from and how to pray
It's first class, *VIP* - Is it fantasy or reality?
It's a booster shot for my self-esteem
For I'm a man among men
Seeking *"The American Dream"*

What is a man without a dream? He's like a tide without a shore, it rolls right along seeking, but finding no end. Well, here's to sand between your toes, being prayed up, keeping hope alive, and either having a view from the top or living large...

"NO MORE LIVING FROM CHECK TO CHECK"

Judge not and you shall not be judged. It's been said that, "first impressions often last forever." Sometimes, we truly live a lifetime trying to live them down. But for all of those who've given up or are giving up on you, let them know that the fat lady hasn't sang yet, nor have you received your final curtain call. Nor have they seen...

"THE FINISHED EFFORT"

If you look at me
And don't see everything
You want to see
Think of your own inhibitions
If you listen to me
And understand what I'm saying
Then evaluate realistically
If I could only find that
And the question is asked again
We all seek something
That will bring us happiness
More than just, now and then
I want to be me
That's all I can be
I am all that you see
When you look at me
But there's more to me
Than that what you see
I am that I am
But I am not all that I want to be
For you see there's a power in me
That makes me want to be better
I am seemingly one who takes loose ends
And tie them together
And really believe the finished effort will be better

Heroes have been found in what were previously determined **lesser men**. And geniuses, artists and statesmen have come forth from those others deemed would never amount to anything.

Take it from **The Poet,** with each day comes "potential."
"THERE'S MORE TO ME THEN THAT WHAT YOU SEE"

The world is filled with visionaries, wanderers and dreamers. It's been said many times that "the worth of a man is measured by the failures or successes of his dreams." But I caution you to evaluate that which is considered success. For sometimes, reaching a peak is almost as rewarding as reaching the summit, and by celebrating small successes, we learn to appreciate the breath of the dream. And, therefore, it becomes the norm to be...

"CHASING AFTER A DREAM"

I'm chasing after a dream
I once had to put on hold
Bringing back to life a thought
That once was my goal
I'm just a dreamer, they say, and it seems
But my Reality depends upon my Dreams
There'll be those who'll tell you that
Dreams don't come true
But with this "Dream" (that I have)
I'll prove that they do
How often times I've thought, it was a near lost cause
Caught up in "Society's Role," governed by its Laws
But hard work, sacrifice and time
Has brought me full circle, to this dream of mine
Now I'm looking forward to proving something I always knew
That "dreams do come true"

The world is filled with dreamers. I'm not talking about those with their eyes closed, nor am I talking about daydreamers (they're like window shoppers). I'm talking about those with a vision that's worthy of effort, patience and persistence to achieve. If yours qualify, and you believe in it, reach for your dreams. I only encourage you because of that passion that's in me. And:

"I'M JUST A DREAMER, THEY SAY, AND IT SEEMS"
***
"BUT MY REALITY DEPENDS UPON MY DREAMS"

Have you ever found yourself up to your neck in a daydream or fantasy and shook yourself to get back on track? This old world keeps us running at such a constant pace that we owe it to ourselves every now and then to take a time out.

Well, if you take this poem, memorize and recite it three times in a row in a calm relaxed setting, it just might vent the pressures of the day. It's worked for me quite often and, as a self proclaimed Doctor of Poetry, I highly recommend:

"MEDITATION PROCLAMATION"
(*Remember poetry is not a proven science*)

From a vantage point, atop a rainbow
One can see within one's soul
Check out the mind
Even view a pot of gold
Visualize yourself upon such an ark
Let your mind run free
Meditate on that which is real
With a bit of fantasy
Scope out the world
Not just that which surrounds you

For from atop a rainbow
One has quite a view
Meditate on what you feel, realizing too
That fantasy in reality is a natural part of you
Meditate, meditate, meditate on what you feel
Enjoy your fantasy to its fullest
But don't forget to be for real.

In a time and age where many are taking artificial stimulants to enhance their creativity, ability, presence, awareness, or to just try to fit in, here's a way to relieve the stress in your life with a clear head and focus.

FPA (Federal Poetry Association) Warning:
Unsupervised or structured fantasy can lead to a reality lapse. Do not recite more than recommended.
If stress continues, try once more at a slower, more relaxed pace, or contact your real doctor.

(The medical statements were all an effort of humor by the author and his own opinion)

"THAT FANTASY IN REALITY IS A NATURAL PART OF YOU"

OPPORTUNITY

I've heard it said that "opportunity is a blessing." And, from my perspective, I believe it to be so. For there have been many with the skills and knowledge, but were passed by because they were not blessed with the opportunity to showcase or expound. But to me, the flipside is even worse; that is to be seeking a blessing and not be prepared to receive it when opportunity knocks.

"OPPORTUNITY"

When you're out there searching success in mine
Opportunity is the key that will bring it in line
Knocks on the door may mean opportunity passing by
There's a rule of thumb that you might want to try
No one knows when opportunity will arrive
Telling you in which direction you should strive
What you should do is prepare for that blessed day
You'll be ahead of the game if you do it this way
Find your direction and prepare come what may

It's one thing to have not decided on your goal and an opportunity arises. It's natural to question direction when an early opportunity presents itself. But to have direction, commitment, and perhaps, been out beating the bush, so to speak, we should then have prepared ourselves for the anticipated unexpected opportunity.

"NO ONE KNOWS WHEN OPPORTUNITY WILL ARRIVE"

There it is again staring you right in the face, another multi-phased situation that definitely needs your attention. Whether it's stretching that almighty dollar in the midst of training one of our future leaders, or trying to hold down that job while going to school, whatever the challenge, when success is found in your effort it's such:

"A SWEET SAVOR"

The challenge is more often as a giant among men
Harder to just fend off, let alone win
The test is usually against overwhelming odds
Battle within a battle is where it often starts
The conflict surges and rarely subsides
Sweeter is the effort when success arrives
The fact that you believed and did not waiver
Victory then won is such *"A Sweet Savor"*

Everyday we're challenged and have to match wits within the bounds of our everyday circles. It's a manageable effort most of the time, but every so often when those circles intertwine, we're faced with major challenges just to maintain. Like when three or four efforts begin to become unmanageable, and they collide with the physical, personal, social, political and your spiritual walks of life, but it's then that we learn to balance the scales of fortitude and magnitude.

"THE HARDER THE BATTLE THE SWEETER THE VICTORY"

Somewhere along this walk of life, I crossed paths with what I first deemed an interesting proverb, it loomed as though a beacon in the night. And as my effort to enhance my way of life brought me occasionally, face-to-face with this humongous "bit" of reality, I no longer saw it as a path to cross, but as one of the routes to incorporate in my effort to enhance my way.

It was as the old Chinese response for a good deed done (how can I repay you), "By helping ten others at the same cost."

"A GOOD DEED"

There's always someone in need
No man is an island indeed
Limit reveals the best we can do
To some it's but a hurdle, to others a mountain true
The effort often requires sacrifice, patience and time
Amount varies as necessity defines
Of all the desires that one may heed
Good is the one to help those in need
You shall receive a blessing beyond compare
Can see it in others eyes because they know you care
Do it because you see a need and it need be done
If that is your reasoning may your reward be a special one
You may do something small or something great
Don't always matter the magnitude for it's not judged by weight
Care is measured by appreciation and gratification
Who others look upon with a sense of admiration
Receive it if it comes if not be self-satisfied
The need for help is not appreciation, but a need obliged
Credit the deed and the character of the one fulfilling the need

To be able to is an awesome position to be in. It's a difference between wanting to and can't, being able to and won't, or doing it for a small nominal fee. And surely we shouldn't be too hasty to throw caution aside, for it's a difference in doing a good deed and putting oneself totally in harm's way.

To make a plan and set guidelines for your life is commendable. But wisdom informs that no man is an island, and that it is wise to help others, for we know not when we, or a loved one, may be in need. Then that would be following a basic good line of logic in hopes that one good turn deserves another. But to see a need and desire to assist, without the desire of personal gain or compensation, is to travel the path before you.

"THERE'S NO LIMIT TO THE AMOUNT OF GOOD YOU CAN DO IF YOU; DON'T CARE WHO RECEIVE THE CREDIT"

Decisions, decisions, and more decisions. It's inevitable that we will eventually be challenged to perform in the realm of *yea and nay*. And in making these choices, we then must face the obligations, responsibilities and responses that come with them. But remember some of that old verbiage from a time gone by; you know, no one said it would be easy; *patience wins the race, stay hopeful*, or *stay prayerful*. And when you've done all you can, put it in God's hands and endure yet:

"ANOTHER TEST OF TIME"

Everyday we are asked, encouraged or forced to make choices
Is often tempted by those opposing small wee voices
Another question needs an answer, situation an explanation
Challenge is often made beyond ability or expectation

Yet, we must make a choice or seek a solution
Another decision made at the height of confusion
Test our reaction, will and selection
Of which leads and guides our direction
Time is but a marker marking the decisions of the mine.

It's often, which of these small wee voices or as our elders would say, *"my first mind or my second mind"* that we choose to listen to that determines the magnitude of the challenge we must face. But with each encounter, challenge, and test engaged, we are stronger, wiser and more able to distinguish between those small wee voices.

"EVERYDAY IS ANOTHER CHALLENGE YET ANOTHER TEST OF TIME"

What time is it? It's always time for this or that, or approaching time for the other. And it rarely ever seems like there's enough time to oblige all the needs at the time. So, we go about trying to add hours to an already extended thirty-two hour day, wondering why we're always running short of time, and not accepting the fact that we set the pace or someone else sets it for us. We're off and running, striving through ambition or responsibility to achieve our dreams, goals and ever present deadline that need yesterday's responsibility. Adding to the stress in life and being sentenced or sentencing ourselves to:

"SERVING TIME"

Never enough time for success, always trying to succeed
Never enough time for what you want, always striving for what you need
Never enough time for those you love
Never enough time for *"God"* above
Never enough time for the *"little"* things

Never enough time for *"Big Dreams"*
Never enough time for preaching
Never enough time for teaching
Never enough time for leading, just going with the flow
Never enough time for the present, always living in the future or the past
Never enough time for being first, always just trying to last
Never enough time for enjoying the fulfillment of your dreams
Caught up in society's role and everything in between
Never enough time for understanding the knowledge of the day
Caught up in the rhetoric of life, lost along the way
Time, time, time, time, time, time, time your time, my time, our time, quality time,
This time, that time, last time, next time, sometime, anytime, every time, at no time
What time is it? It's show time, prime time
In time, on time, trying to make time
Out of time because time waits for no one
Time, time, time broken down for many into fifteen minutes of fame
Thinking, hoping, believing, praying someone will remember your name
I haven't got the time, I need more time
Time running out on you, never enough time....
Make the time - take the time - make the time - take the time
Time out -- for—It's - time - to- stop - serving - time.

Chill, take a chill pill if you will (a figure of speech). Clear your plate and reorganize to allow time for the real deal. You know, like some quality time for those you love, for God above, and for every now and then enjoying the wonder of you. Now, this isn't about adding to the need for more time, this is about removing some of the things that monopolize your time which aren't worth your time.

"TIME OUT- - FOR - - IT'S - -TIME - -TO - - STOP- - SERVING - - TIME"

SUNSET

I REMEMBER... *A Dedication To The Poet*

The Poet. My Father. An Example. A Role Model.

I remember the day my Mother left our family. You would have thought someone died with all of the company we had in our home. Family members came and offered their sympathy and each family member offered to raise one of *The Poet's* children. They assumed he could not possibly raise three small children under the age of seven by himself. But my Father refused to give up his parental rights and custody because he did not want to break up his family. *The Poet* was a strong man just like his Father.

I remember *The Poet* preaching to me on just about every subject. *The Poet* should have been a preacher, as much as he preached, which is why his next book will be titled '*The Poet and The Preacher.*' I heard a sermon everyday before I went to school. And those same sermons are being preached to my daughter, Alivia.

I remember when I was in the Ms. Covert Pageant in 1988, I pulled a question from the hat and it read, "Who is the most inspirational person in your life?" I paused because at that moment I was overwhelmed with my response, which was on the tip of my tongue. And my answer to that question was my Father, Charles Edward Peterson, Sr., because he instilled within me a can do attitude and he was a role model within our community. Of course, I came in 1st runner-up for the competition, but in my Father's eyes, I was a Queen.

I remember *The Poet* going through many hard times and disappointments. And, I know at times, my stubbornness has made *The Poet* become disappointed in me. *The Poet* was a very strict man and everyone knew not to bother his children. And, I on many occasions was considered spoiled, because *The Poet* was always on someone's case about me. But, I am my Father's child; I am stubborn just like *The Poet*.

I remember seeing *The Poet* cry for the first time at my sister, Tanisha's, funeral. I began to look at my Father in a different light. I no longer considered him an invincible man; but a man filled with love for his children.

I remember my Father staying at home and playing Monopoly with his children, shuttling his children between cheerleading and basketball practice, and writing at night and placing his poetry inside his Blue Trunk. *The Poet* didn't hang out on the street corners, drink alcohol, or party; *The Poet* worked very hard to support his family as a single parent.

I remember when *The Poet's* close high school friend took us to church. We were so happy to be in the company of other children besides school. After that, my siblings and I begged our Father to take us to church and he agreed. It was during this time he placed his life *Back In God's Hands*. Soon, *The Poet* was a deacon, male chorus member and church trustee. And, I also remember when *The Poet* placed his life *Back In God's Hands*; he was blessed with a great paying job, which he still works today. God is so merciful.

I remember *The Poet* walking seven miles everyday to go to work, no matter how adverse the weather was in our small town of Covert, Michigan. *The*

Poet would chop wood in freezing cold weather, and build a fire in our fireplace for those times when the oilman didn't come to fill our tank. I am very proud of my Father. *HE* is more than a role model. *HE* is a mentor and a motivator. *HE* is an inspiration, and *HE* has left a legacy for his children's children. I applaud *The Poet* for his tenacity, perseverance, and leadership abilities. I love him!

Anita Shari Peterson

The Poet's First Born

THE POET'S PERSPECTIVE

"Didn't I Tell you there'd be a test"?

1. Which Perspective complemented the poem best for you?
2. Can you say your ABC's - twice?
3. Are you still going in "Circles?
4. Do you think that you may have caught a glimpse of "THE WATCHER"?
5. Did you learn the true value of "A Good Deed"?
6. Did you learn the meanings of Abstain and Father?
7. Can you understand "It Is Not Enough"?
8. Whom can you tell to "Weigh The Cost"?
9. Can you encourge or prevent someone from suffering " Hard Times"?
10."What Will It Take" to turn your "Dreams" into "Reality"?

The Poet's Perspective
Platinum Collector's Edition

ORDER FORM

Here's How To Order A Copy: Or Even Better -- Several Copies

Electronic Mail Orders (E-Mail): orders@pcgpublishing.com

Postal Orders: PCG Publishing Company

C/O Order Fulfillment

60407 M-43 Hwy

Bangor, MI 49013

USA

269-427-2068

Web Orders: PCG Publishing Company Accepts Credit Cards Via

www.pcgpublishing.com

For assistance via e-mail, please send a message: orders@pcgpublishing.com

---

The Poet's Perspective -- *Platinum Edition*

Quantity Ordered: _____

CUSTOMER INFORMATION:

NAME: _____

ADDRESS 1: _____

ADDRESS 2: _____

City/State/Zip: _____

Telephone Number: _____

Cost Per Unit: $14.95 + 2.95 Shipping and Handling

Sales Tax: Please add 6% for products shipped to Michigan Address

Special Requests / Comments:

_____

_____

_____

Would you like to be added to our mailing list?

Yes: Please provide e-mail address

_____

No: Not right now

Special Requests: Circle All That Apply

Sign My Book

Visit My City

Speaking Engagement Request

Whether you are saying goodbye to a friend or loved one or expressing your desire to see someone succeed. Maybe there is the need for encouragement, and you want to let some one know that they are never alone. Then you might want to tell them:

"I WISH YOU WELL"

MAY the blessings of the day be within your reach

THE knowledge to learn as well as to teach

SADDEST moments on do not dwell

DAY will come in which you shall prevail

OF all the things that your heart desire

YOUR dreams will help to take you higher

FUTURE accomplishments that you'll achieve

BE thru the avenue of faith if you'll just believe

NO one is exempt from the trials of time

WORSE come to worse caught up in a bind

THEN when it's clearly out of your control

THE "Spirit" helps you to achieve your goal

HAPPIEST is the one who finds peace of mind

DAYS of pleasure lived by design

OF all the things you can possess

YOUR happiness and peace of mind is the best

PAST, present, and future, intertwine to manage the process of time

And maybe, just maybe, The Poet's Perspective has enlightened, educated, and uplifted you so that you may consider this book to be the best (or one of the best) poetry books you have ever read. And with that being said, "I Wish You Well."

I come to you in the volume of the book with purpose, as one crying in the wilderness "trying to open the eyes of the children of man before they are harvested by minds of destruction. For God sent Preachers, God sent Teachers, God sent Prophets and God sent Poets.

And I am THE POET and this is *The Poet's Perspective.*

Printed in the United States
46553LVS00009B/61-114

9 780977 254149